ORIGIN
OF
DUTY AND RIGHT.

THE
ORIGIN
OF
DUTY AND RIGHT
IN
MAN,
CONSIDERED.

ἩΜΩΝ ΤΟ ΠΟΛΙΤΕΥΜΑ ΕΝ ΟΥΡΑΝΟΙΣ ΥΠΑΡΧΕΙ.
PHIL. III. V. 20.

LONDON:

PRINTED BY J. BATESON, DENMARK-STREET, FOR
RICHARD WHITE,
PICCADILLY.
1796.

ADDRESSED

TO

THE INHABITANTS

OF

LONDON AND WESTMINSTER

ON THE

APPROACHING PROGRESS

OF THE

KING

TO

THE PARLIAMENT.

—— " That thou may'st beware
" By what is past."
PAR. LOST, VI. 894.

WE here lay claim, in limine *of our Address, to the candid judgment of that respectable Body to whom we have ventured to present it; lest the compass into which we have attempted to reduce so extensive a subject, and the haste with which it has been unavoidably drawn up, and of which it carries with it but too many evidences, may in parts have rendered the performance involved.*

If, however, we should have the good fortune to discover, by their suffrage, that the view we have taken of the great questions of DUTY *and* RIGHT *as subsisting in* MAN, *is just; and that the thread of our argument, however it may be* involved, *is yet* unbroken;

broken; *we might be tempted at a future day to elucidate that view, and to develope that argument, detached from the peculiar, accidental matter, which has occasioned our submitting it to their notice at this particular time.*

April 26, 1796.

THE ORIGIN OF DUTY AND RIGHT IN MAN CONSIDERED.

Addressed to the Inhabitants of London and Westminster, &c. &c.

THE Time is nearly at hand, when the King will proceed, in discharge of the high function vested in him by the Constitution, to meet the Lords and Commons of Great Britain, assembled in Parliament.

Whatever the occasion is capable of presenting to a contemplative mind, in the perfect equipoise it exhibits of the interests and duties of associated man, yet, from long use, and familiar enjoyment of the blessings derived from the Constitution, it would have but little expectation to arrest the observation of Englishmen at this particular time, were it not for circumstances the most afflictive, if not the most portentous, that have disturbed the nation's internal quiet since the æra of the

Revolution; that brilliant æra, in which the interests of the British people were secured, the prices of liberty and good government ascertained, and the balance of the state finally adjusted, by the limits assigned to the powers, privileges, and prerogatives of the three constituent branches of the Legislature.

The circumstances here alluded to, are of a date too recent, and of a quality too impressive, and having moreover taken place within the limits of YOUR residence, are of a notoriety too general, to impose the hateful task of rehearsing them. These, however, are the circumstances, that render the approaching progress of the King to the Parliament an object of peculiar interest to the great body of the nation; and that occasion, which, until the insinuation of the political venom of France had deranged the equable system of British society, commanded always its natural and becoming portion of respect, without exciting any extraordinary emotion, now rouses the attention of the whole family of Britons, dispersed throughout the empire: Who, reflecting with horror upon the dreadful phenomenon of civil guilt exhibited at the time of the last Royal progress, anticipate with anxiety the return of that event; and, at the same time, direct their eyes upon
YOU,

YOU, THE INHABITANTS OF LONDON AND WESTMINSTER, whom the local arrangements neceſſary to regular ſociety, and the political and commercial intereſts of the Britiſh Empire, have rendered the depoſits and natural guardians of the Legiſlature of your country.

The proſpect of this event, acquires thus, from a retroſpective view of the inſults that the King then ſuſtained, an intereſt unequalled alas! in the annals of the kingdom, becauſe unequalled in its cauſe; and it places YOU in a ſituation the moſt critical, as being conjured by the voice of your countrymen, to prevent the attachment of that ſtain which might adhere to the Britiſh name from the monſtrous enormities then committed. And becauſe the laws of man's nature, which confine his perſonal exertions to ſo narrow a ſphere, render it impoſſible for each to concur with his individual ſuccour towards obtaining that end; they, therefore, look for it from YOU, who ſhare in the principles and feelings common to Engliſhmen, and who, excluſively of YOUR own particular intereſts concerned, are juſtly held to owe this to YOUR fellow-countrymen diſtributed in the kingdom, in return for the diſtinguiſhed advantages, which YOUR proximity to the Legiſlature, and the other circumſtances of YOUR ſituation, neceſſarily confer.

Upon these considerations alone, therefore, that the nation looks back with horror on the late assaults offered to the person of the Sovereign; and that being unable individually to display either their detestation of those acts, or their attachment to the office, or person of the King; or to concert measures for expelling from within YOUR residence, the infernal cause of enormities endangering the fabric of our liberties, they look with passionate confidence to YOU, to discharge the peculiar duties resulting from YOUR local situation: upon these considerations only, the present address is urged; in which, whether we fail, or whether we succeed, no sound and upright mind—no pure and unaccusing conscience, will suspect any other purpose to be at heart, than that of aiding to stem the career of principles disseminated throughout the nation, but no where with so much activity, so much address, so much calculation, and, alas! so much success, as in the large and populous metropolis of which YOU are THE INHABITANTS. Principles, acting in direct opposition to every admitted and approved principle of civil subordination, every instruction of social experience, every light of reason and religion; principles, whose immediate operation it is, to eradicate every particle of attachment to the existing Constitution, whether we received that attachment

tachment by inheritance, or derived it from a contemplative survey of the blessings we have so long, and so effectually, continued to possess; and, creating a nausea or disgust towards it, from the very cause which entitles it more than any other to our affectionate esteem, namely, its long duration: that is to say, not that decrepid age which enfeebles and wears out the springs of action; but that confirmed solidity, which, accumulating proof upon proof of its superior aptness to answer every end of civil government, establishes on a basis, immoveable by reason, its constant and invariable excellence.

On YOU, then, as proxies for the British People to proclaim their sentiments—on YOU, whose name the demon of treason has endeavoured, by an infernal artifice, to involve in her own infamy; a duty of this lofty nature is imposed. And it is with a consoling confidence that we look for the conduct YOU shall pursue, to disarm malevolence of even the shadow of a reason for insinuating, that either by favour, or through cowardice, an assault was suffered to take place, and moreover to be repeated, upon the person of the Chief Magistrate, in the heart of YOUR residence, and, therefore, in the focus of YOUR abilities. For malice will not be unwatchful of the opportunity afforded,

afforded, should YOU seem not to have reflected on those enormities with that salutary horror, which shall determine YOU to use the pregnant experience of the past, in regulating the events of the future; and in striving to prevent a repetition of the effects, by endeavouring, with every means consistent with your civil duties, to extinguish or to incapacitate the energy of the cause.

If we look for the most general cause of that internal disquiet, which at length broke forth into the scenes now under contemplation, we may venture, without odium, to express it by the general name of, discontent: by which we mean an uneasiness under existing circumstances, with a desire of producing a change in them. Such a mood, when considered as existing in any considerable part of a large community, will vary its degree in respect to those circumstances, or, which is the same thing in its effect, in respect to the view that the mind takes of those circumstances. For, as the passions of man are roused and called out into action in consequence of the impressions received by the mind; and, as the human mind is ever liable to admit erroneous impressions, there can be no doubt that erroneous impressions once conveyed to the mind, will produce real passions, and all the

consequences of real passions, as effectually as true impressions could do. All causes of discontent to existing circumstances, if they are founded in truth, will act upon all who are in the same common situation, and who possess a common nature, and discontent will be immediately and necessarily produced in each. When then the discontent originates only in a few, and is only extended progressively to the numbers, through the mediation and industry of the few, it is clear that the numbers are not immediately impressed by causes existing in nature, but mediately through the instrumentality of the few in whom discontent has taken place: and, as such partial discontent cannot proceed from general causes affecting each, otherwise each would be affected by them, but is personal and original in the individuals themselves; the discontent that they communicate to others, is only the diffusion or propagation of their own discontent. But as men are only to be actuated by a sense, or persuasion of interest, and therefore take part with others, only in proportion as they conceive themselves concerned in their acting; so the numbers can only be induced to concur with the few, by an apprehension raised in their minds that they have interests involved or at stake; and the impression not being received from nature, but being produced by the
in-

industry of men, labouring under a discontented mind, and who can only reach the moral organ of those in whom they endeavour to excite discontent, through the organ of the fancy, or that part of the mind which receives the impressions by which the passions are raised; it is clear that such an impression derives its origin, not from the nature of the case, but from the subtilty and interest of the few, who are thus the source and conduit of the discontent; and consequently that it is not founded in truth, but in illusion and error.

The nature and object of the discontent, therefore, varies in relation to those in whom it subsists; who may be said to be of two descriptions; those in whom it originates, and those to whom it is derived; or, in more popular and ordinary phrase, *the leaders*, and *the led*. The discontent of the former differs in its original from that of the latter; as the first arises from a principle of self-will, the second from a principle of error. There is, however, a peculiar subtilty and virulence in the nature of this error, that renders the transition from error to guilt rapid and complete. So that unless the malady be stopped in its early stage of error, it speedily alters its quality, and may soon advance to every degree of turpitude and malignity.

To remove this discontent, or to nullify its activity, requires a difference of process, according to the principle from which it proceeds, or according to the state in which it subsists. That which subsists as a principle of self-will, demands the steady and inflexible coercion of justice; that which subsists as a principle of error, claims every aid and succour that mercy and wisdom can impart. The first rouses in us a sentiment of the most unqualified indignation and disgust; the second, while it diffuses a melancholy upon the mind, awakens in us a sentiment of a very opposite nature.

Of the two descriptions of persons here considered, the latter are infinitely the most numerous; and on this, as well as on many other considerations, they challenge our principal regard. The first may be considered, in general, as the efficient, the latter as the instrumental, cause of all our internal disquiet. By wresting the instrument from the hand of crime, we shall strip it of the only means it has for producing its effect. By removing error, therefore, we in a manner paralyse the force of crime. On the other hand, if we take the fullest vengeance of crime, and at the same time take no steps to repair the waste it may have occasioned, the flood of error which it has discharged will stagnate over the surface of the country, and the spawn of crime with which the fluid so plentifully abounds, will sooner or later ripen into life and activity.

To remove, therefore, the discontent of the majority, which proceeds from error, is a measure equally enjoined by wisdom and by charity: by wisdom, as it is the most effectual method to recover ourselves to peace and general confidence; by charity, as it is the only means possible for reinstating others in the capacity of obtaining happiness.

The removal of error may be effected by two different operations, which are thus described by a wise and valuable writer:

" When error prevails, there are two ways by
" which the cause of truth may be maintained;
" either by a direct and formal refutation of the
" error, or by a plain and effectual establishment
" of the truth.

" The advocate for truth may descend into
" the field of controversy, he may engage every
" adversary that comes in his way, he may pursue
" and expose every single error. But error pos-
" sesses a wide and dark dominion, and he who
" undertakes the conquest of the whole, under-
" takes

" takes a labour that is almoſt infinite. It will
" ſtill find ſome obſcure corner to retire to, from
" which it will be found hard to diſpoſſeſs it.

" There is another way of removing error, and
" that is, by a full and clear expoſition of the
" truth. There is ſomething much more pleaſing
" to a liberal mind in the eſtabliſhment of truth,
" than in the refutation of error; as the labour is
" more pleaſing to rear a fair and well-proportioned
" edifice, than to pull down one that is miſhapen
" and ill-proportioned *."

The mode of combating error, recommended by this excellent writer, is that which we feel ourſelves ſtrongly impelled to attempt under the authority of YOUR name, and in the opportunity that we have ſought for in this addreſs; and perhaps it will hardly be found in any caſe ſo entirely deſirable, as in the great and comprehenſive queſtion, which we ſhall now endeavour to conſider.

If we examine the complexion of that diſcontent which has of late produced ſo much alarm and diſ-quiet amongſt us; if we conſider the period of its origin, and the circumſtances of its progreſs, we

* Rotheram's *Essay on Faith*, Pref.

shall have no difficulty in discovering that it has relation to a question that has been turned and shaped into a variety of forms, adapted to every taste, prejudice, and capacity of man, but still expressed by the same phrase—*the Rights of Man*.

The *manner* in which this question was brought forward before the public mind being *new*, a scandalous and too successful use was made of this *novelty* of the *mode* to persuade a *novelty* of the *subject:* and because the question of the rights of mankind, viewed in respect of human government to which they were confided, and of Almighty God, from whom they were originally derived, had been hitherto conducted in a manner totally different from that which was then introduced, it was basely and wickedly pretended that they had never been investigated at all; that they were objects of truth, newly exposed to the perception of the intellect by the blaze of French philosophy; and that, as they formed a body of important interests inseparable from the nature of man, but till then unknown in Britain, it was necessary that Englishmen also should direct every faculty of mind, every energy of passion, towards this alluring object, and break in upon an establishment by which they were precluded from obtaining it. Such was the dishonest and insidious artifice employed by the authors of the discontent, to propagate the spirit by which they were moved; and by the general diffusion of which only they could hope to attain to those objects, to which their passions so resolutely tended.

It is a lamentable reflection, that there should have been found Englishmen so abject and degenerate, as for a moment to yield themselves the dupes of so gross and shameless a falshood! that they should so soon have lost sight of the eminence on which their ancestors have stood for upwards of a century, and on which they themselves were nursed: that they, who were to France the original archetype of liberty, and who first showed her the practical enjoyment of man's best rights, should be imbecil enough to suffer her to pluck this fairest feather from the British plume, and insultingly implant it in her own red cap: that, after boasting of the glorious Revolution for upwards of an hundred years, they should consent to be told by France that the Revolution was *not glorious*, that it was only a modification of tyranny, founded on principles now become dangerous and obsolete, and which must no longer be tolerated in Europe: and that they should have given France credit for a calumny so outrageous. Melancholy, indeed, is the reflection upon this truth!

What,

What, alas! would be the feelings of our illustrious ancestors, those to whom many generations of a just and grateful posterity have ascribed the blessings of the freedom and security they have enjoyed, could they quit their tombs, and behold, in the present age thousands of their servile descendants, vying with each other to surrender up to France the fairest honours of England, and to concede the palm, long since adjudged to themselves, to a Paine, a St. Just, or a Roberspierre!

If we look to that arrogant and savage instructress, we shall perceive that she commenced her doctrines with a boisterous clamour of the rights of man; rights, indeed, of the most sacred and important nature to mankind, but which were never worse understood, nor worse promoted, than in her school: and from this school of distraction comes forth an apostle of treason and blasphemy, an apostate from this his illustrious and insulted country, and dares to bring forward the question of the rights of mankind as a question new to Englishmen and unconsidered by the British Constitution; in which, whether consummate ignorance or villany prevail, YOU are well able to decide. For, if that libeller does not know, that the history of the English nation is the

history

history of man's best rights gradually rising into fruit, but proceeding with that deliberation which ever marks the progress of wisdom*; if he does not know, that at the glorious æra of 1688, the rights of man were better considered, better ascertained, and better confirmed in relation to reason, experience and religion, than at any other period before or since; in that case, consummate ignorance prevails: but if, knowing all this, he nevertheless denies it, conceals it, misrepresents it, so as to effect the dark purpose of betraying the confi-

---

* The cautious, and often in appearance the tardy process of wisdom, is obvious to the perception of every wise and observing mind. " *Ne souhaitons jamais de Révolution ; plaignons nos peres de celles qu' ils ont éprouvées. Le bien, dans la nature physique et morale, ne descend du ciel sur nous que lentement, peu-à-peu, j' ai presque dit goutte à goutte ; mais tout ce qui est subit, instantané, tout ce qui est révolution, est une source de maux.*"—— " Let us never wish for revolution; let us compassionate our forefathers for those they have undergone. Good, both natural and moral, is only transmitted from heaven to us slowly, by little and little,—I had almost said, drop by drop; but all that is sudden, instantaneous, all that is strictly revolution, is a source of calamities." These memorable words are those of the unfortunate BAILLY, which he expressed in the January of the year 1778. How justly he spoke, he himself illustriously witnessed, when—at once an instrument and victim of the very convulsion he had deprecated—he expired under the guillotine at Paris in the year 1794.——See *Lettres sur L'Atlantide de Platon*, &c. p. 21.

dence

dence of an inquiring multitude, and of perverting the principles on which is established the happiness of a great people, in order that he may raise himself to eminence on the mound of ruin he shall occasion, then is he discharged from the imputation of ignorance; but it is only that he may receive that of the most hardened treachery, and deepest malignity, that man in the bosom of society is capable of conceiving.

In attempting to counteract the fatal effects of that error which, by means of this question, has been rendered fruitful of those dreadful scenes which so lately disgraced the capital, it is not our intention (as we have already said) to descend into that intricate wild into which the inquiry has been purposely and craftily drawn by those who assert its novelty, or to pursue all the various crossings and by-paths, through which the failing adversary escapes to present himself afresh on some new ground; thus rendering the contest, like skirmishes with banditti in a forest, interminable and ineffectual. Such a process is foreign to our present design; which is, to co-operate, to the best of our feeble ability, with the exertions YOU shall make in defence of truth and order, by endeavouring to acquire and to communicate

cate * a clear and diftinct impreffion of the truth on which this great queftion refts; fince, if what we fhall fubmit fhould be fo fortunate as to eftablifh conviction, every contrary argument will at once, by this fimple operation, ftand virtually refuted.

The queftion of the rights of man, which of late has engaged the genius of fo many different cafts of philofophers, is not only of a nature fo important, but is alfo of an appearance fo feductive, that every fair and upright inquirer, whofe primary object is the attainment of truth, will obferve the progrefs of the argument with more than ordinary jealoufy; left the allurements of perfonal intereft, which this queftion appears to offer with fuch unbounded profufion, fhould enfeeble the force of truth, and his judgment receive a bias contrary to that fide, which, if the argument prefented fewer attractions, his reafon would decidedly incline him to.

Although the authoritative movers of the controverfy have endeavoured to preclude all examina-

---

* " Exiftimabam enim pro veritate non nifi veritate certandum, et quidem tali quam ipfe animo approbarem : fruftra enim daturum me operam, ut perfuaderem aliis, quæ non ante mihi perfuafiffem."———Grotius, *De Verit*. I. i. c. 1.

tion into the nature and origin of *right*, by assuming that part of the question as settled, yet as this assumption becomes thus the first principle on which they rest what they are pleased to call "the eternal and imprescriptible rights of man," they leave their argument to rest ultimately on the general question of right. To the nature and origin of right, therefore, we shall direct our first attention; and if it should presently appear that every right in man must have *an origin*, and may have *an end*, the pretension to *eternity* in those rights (which is essential to the establishment of their argument) will be at once destroyed: and a cautious mind will, from this single circumstance, prepare itself to view with suspicion and doubt, every other pretension, however plausible, that the same argument may endeavour to establish.

In examining into the question of the *rights of man*, it is first of all necessary to ascertain and fix the signification of those words, that the argument may not stray away into perplexity, merely for the want of a sufficient accuracy of guidance at the outset. It is necessary, therefore, to observe, that those words—*the rights of man*—comprehend two distinct objects, each demanding a distinct and full investigation: the first being an inquiry *What is a right?* the second an inquiry, *What is man?*

which

which questions being solved, we shall then, and then only, be able to arrive at the conclusion aimed at, and be qualified to pronounce, what are the *rights of man.*

The question that first meets us, and as it were barrs the progress to all further inquiry is, what is *a right?* To this a satisfactory answer must be given, before we can advance another step in the territory of truth. But the answer is easily given. Every notion of *a right,* is a notion of *a title* or *just claim* * to the use, or possession, of *something.* He who alleges *a right,* must produce *a title*; he must, in the language of our courts, *show cause* why that alleged right is to stand, and why it may not be invaded. *A right* is a *title* founded, not upon assertion, but upon a producible proof; it depends entirely upon evidence; a right, therefore, in its most general and comprehensive sense, denotes that solid and fundamental reason,†on which a claimant can justly assume any benefit to himself, and at the same time resist any operation tending to deprive him of that benefit.

A title is defined by Sir Edward Coke to be, " *a just cause* for possessing &c." Titulus est *justa*

---

* Jacob's Law Dict.   Johnson's Dict.

† " Non tantum ut *vires cogendi* habeat, sed etiam ut *justas* habeat *causas vindicandi.* &c." Leibniz.

causa possidendi *id* quod *nostrum est.*"* This is exactly what the mind intends when it speaks of *a right*; being its universal nature, whether it respects civil or natural objects. And yet we cannot but observe the equivocation to which the popular use of the word *right* is liable,† namely, that, it is used all at once to signify both the *just cause*, or ground of claim, and also *the object* itself sought for by that claim. For both in their turns are called *a right*. Thus it is popularly said, that " man *has* a natural *right to* life," and again, that " *life is* a natural *right* of man;" and yet in the first of these propositions the word *right* denotes a *title*, or what Sir Ed. Coke calls, the just cause or ground, " *justa causa* possidendi ;" and in the second it denotes the *object* of a title, or what the same authority calls " *id quod* nostrum est." To discriminate between these two considerations, is of very material consequence towards a faithful and correct management of the argument of right; so that in which ever of these two senses the word *right* is at any time first employed, in that sense only it ought to be continued throughout; otherwise the confusion

---

* See Blackstone, B. ii. c. 13.
† The indistinctness, and therefore the ambiguity, of the notions affixed to the words *right*, and *jus*, is not confined merely to common and colloquial phraseology; which occasioned the profound Leibniz to remark; " Juris et Justitiæ notiones, etiam " post tot præclaros scriptores, nescio an satis liquidæ habeantur." Leibnizii Op. *Jurisp.* T. iv. p. 294. P. III.

of the two significations, will produce a net-work of perplexity and cross-reasoning, similar to that which the enemies of the truth have exerted so much ingenuity and industry to weave. Consistently with what has been said, are the words of Dr. Taylor; who, speaking of right, observes, that it " is a *moral quality annexed to a person*, enabling him " to have or to do *something justly*." * Now, " *the* " *moral quality annexed to the person*" is the right, and the " *something* that he may have, or do, just-" ly," is the *object* of that right, but is not the right itself. Whatever therefore may be the *object* of the moral quality of right in any particular instance, the moral quality must precede it; he who asserts a right, must prove the existence of the *moral quality* to be annexed to him; which gives him a *moral power* over that which he claims, and establishes a *moral necessity*, or obligation, to submit to that power.† This is the necessary and universal nature of a right.

To establish right on general assertion, to provide it no more solid foundation than the peremptory decision of self-interest, is to withdraw from it the stable basis of reason, and to leave it on the

fluctuating

---

* Elements of Civ. Law.

† " —dicitur, *qualitas moralis*. Ut autem qualitas realis in or-
" dine ad actionem duplex est; *potentia agendi*, et *necessitas agen-*
" *di* ; ita potentia moralis dicitur *jus*, necessitas moralis dicitur
" *obligatio*." Leibniz. *Method: nov: disc: Jurisp.* T. iv. p. 185.

fluctuating and treacherous surface of fancy and of passion. In the late broils concerning the rights of man, the existence of right is assumed; it is no where brought to proof. It is taken for granted in a gratuitous proposition, on which the whole superstructure is raised; and as the architects who compounded it proceeded rapidly in their work, in order to cover in and conceal the nature of the base on which they were building, it will follow that the system so laid and so erected, will be a compound of error and defect. If it be asked, what is the nature or ground of man's right to life, for example, it would be a strange reply to say that it *is* his right; and yet on no better foundation are the insidious systems spread amongst the multitude, and impressed with the character of *the rights of man*, made to depend. But, praised be God, every right that man can claim, is founded on a reason comprehensible by our understandings, distinct in its origin, and defined in its extent; a reason that need not shun inquiry, nor bury itself under an assertion; a reason that need not doubt its ability to substantiate the evidence required, nor seek to augment its authority by courting the vociferation of a multitude. For, right has no sort of dependance upon man's asseveration. Millions of men cannot create a truth; they might become organs delivering a true or a false proposition, but they could not confer a grain of verity on a false proposition,

nor

nor add a grain of verity to a true one. They might express a fixed determination on their part, to act in uniform opposition to the evidence of truth; they might make a solemn and formal covenant, that henceforward the word *right* should bear their new construction; and they might employ their collective force to reduce, or prevent, any opposition to their determination; but still the nature of things would remain unaltered; and right and truth would continue to be just what they were, though there should survive no human mind either capable or willing to acknowledge them.

But the nature of right is founded in what spirits of that temper sedulously avoid, namely, a distinct, producible proof; and it derives no accession of strength whatever from that on which they would wholly rest it, namely, positive assertion. It is the genuine offspring of that eternal and immutable reason, to which all things are subjected, and which has determined their qualities, and prescribed their operations.

As the system of Atheism, notwithstanding the vigorous efforts made in its favour, has not yet impugned the ancient belief of a one sovereign Creator, cause of every thing existing, and of every relation between those things, it is evident that

the

the only original and underived title, the only absolute and underived right, is in Him*; and that every other notion of right, inasmuch as it includes an idea of derivation, either immediately from Him, or mediately through the principles of justice which He has implanted, depends ultimately on that sovereign cause, is essentially referrable to it, and cannot even hypothetically be considered distinctly from it; since it has the whole ground or reason of its existence in the supreme determining reason, by which all things were ordained, and by which only they can be explained.

All right must, therefore, be derived, or underived; and no right can be derived, but from a cause capable of devolving it. Every cause devolving right, must either have it inherently in itself, or must have have received it from some ultimate cause in which it inherently resides. In examining, therefore, into the nature of right, as an indispensable preliminary to the question of the rights of man, we perceive that we are obliged to distinguish between *right derived*, and *right unde-*

---

* " Deus est subjectum juris summi in omnia, nullius vero
" obligationis." Leibniz. Vol. iv. p. 185. P. II. " God is
" the subject in whom sovereign and universal right resides, and
" who is therefore free from all obligation."

rived; and thus, in order to comprehend its nature, to ascend to the governing reason of the universe.

Every right, therefore, that of the Creator alone excepted, is a derived right, flowing from Him as the great Proprietor of all things; and it acquires its quality of right from this only, that it is a title conferred by him, whose right to confer is incontestible.* Such is the original source, the ultimate reason, of all derived right; but it is a reason that

* We are here inquiring after that inherent right, which is supposed to be annexed to every man's common nature, at its origin, antecedently to society, and to all artificial forms of polity received among men. Such a right is widely different from that which was so strenuously maintained in the last century, when the spirit of Jacobitism (closer of kin than the world are aware, to its near namesake of the present day) calculating its interests on the side of monarchical tyranny, as its successor in the present age has done on the side of democratical tyranny, endeavoured to establish the divine right of kings. It is amusing to observe, what different effects one and the same general principle can produce. Both have endeavoured to fix a form of *civil* polity, on a ground of *divine* or *natural* right; this is the principle common to both. The *divine indefeasible* right to *monarchy*, and the *natural indefeasible* right to *democracy*, being notions of the same identica intrinsic quality; and differing only in the application, according to different tastes and interests. For *natural* and *divine* are terms (if they have any meaning at all) of the same *radical* signification, and neither of them in any sense applicable to any artificial form of polity.

has been carefully suppressed by the movers of the controversy, because it would prescribe bounds to a question which they are desirous of leaving open and undefined, and because it would be attended with the inconvenience of raising the mind to a contemplation of the source of right, an elevation that would unavoidably induce a mood, unfavourable to the pursuit of right, after the manner of France. To avoid this, they have industriously spread a veil over the origin of the notion of right; they have choked the way to the principle of right by a mound of stubborn assertion; they have directed the mind to that assertion as to the *ne plus ultra* of inquiry; and they have seduced the unwary or profligate minds of their auditors to believe, that that which is only a proposition capable of proof, but destitute of all authority till proved, is a self-evident proposition; in order that they might not perceive the differences produced by the different modes of employing the proposition, and which would lead the mind to conclusions directly contrary.

Such also is the sacred principle which they have dared to allege, who have deluged Europe with blood; who have taken up arms against the religion of Christendom; who have computed the comfort of any given generation of mankind as a cypher

cypher in the speculations of their philosophies; and such also has been the pretext of their miserably deluded adherents, whose black and flagitious, but by God's providence abortive, endeavours, have lately brought dishonour upon the metropolis.

Was the notion of right as industriously united with its origin, as it has been industriously disunited from it; was that connexion as carefully preserved, as it has been sedulously effaced; was the reason of man faithfully informed in all those things which are only used to disturb his imagination, and to inflame his passions; the question of right would be an inquiry as productive of good to the moral and civil interests of society, as it is now rendered luxuriant in mischief. Did an appeal to the rights of man convey the mind at once into the presence of the moral Governor of the world, the pursuit of those rights would be conducted with that regard to his laws, and to the various duties of man, that would insure the peace and prosperity of society. It would be a process of caution and virtuous sacrifice, not of violence and intemperate avidity; a regard to the duties we might transgress, would correct our attachment to the interests we might promote; conscience and reason would effectually control the operation of crime; and craft and violence, insolence and sedition, treason and

anarchy

anarchy, would no longer be found on the side where the assertion of those rights was professed, but only on that where they were resisted.

We have seen that right, in general, is a notion of title, or just claim; that every title stands upon its documents or proofs, and that none can be admitted till its validity has been examined and recognized; that every right save that of the Creator is deducible from Him, as the only source of right, because the only source of being, and consequently of every attribute of being, of which this of right is one. As then we have ascertained the nature of right wherever it subsists, before we can pronounce what is the specific right annexed to man's nature, or rather what are the specific objects to which the moral power of right in man has respect, it will be necessary to inquire whether any such moral quality is *really* annexed to man, and how it is discoverable; and then we may proceed to determine, what is its extent, and what are its natural objects. And let us banish the sordid fear that would deter us from so noble an investigation, or fill us with the criminal dread of thus finding ourselves reasoned out of right. Truth can never be the object of alarm to any but a distempered or a distorted mind; but of all investigations, least have we to fear from this, from which we shall return without comparison richer, than from the lawless and marauding excursion, into which the buccaneers of the rights of man, have inveigled their incautious retainers. What the excellent Blackstone has remarked of the ordinary conduct of mankind with respect to the notion of the right of property, may be extended to their notion of right in general. " There is nothing (says he) " which so generally strikes the imagination, and " engages the affections of mankind, as the right " of property.—And yet there are very few, that " will give themselves the trouble to consider the " original and foundation of this right. Pleased as " we are with the possession, we are afraid to look " back to the means by which it was acquired, as " if fearful of some defect in our title."* Discarding then a terror of so ungracious and suspicious a quality, let us boldly inquire after the evidence of our right.

As God is the only source of right that reason or common sense can recognise; and as man is a subject to whom a right is capable of being annexed; we are to inquire whether any right flowing from that Source, does *in fact* attach upon that subject, producing *a right in man:* which necessarily brings

* Blackstone's Com. B. II. p. 2.

us to the examination of the subject himself, or in other words to the second object of our inquiry, *what is man?* since it is only by the solution of this question that we can assertain the several properties and relations of man, and by that means discover whether the relation of *right* constitutes any part of the circumstances of his nature.

In defining man, it is unnecessary to be very minute; we are all sufficiently instructed in his origin and nature. We shall therefore only state, that man is a rational and intellectual being, whose present form of existence upon earth is of a limited and short duration; that he is a free agent, having the power of controlling the activity, and determining the tendency of the passions, by which his nature is moved towards the objects necessary for its wellbeing. That he is formed with a capacity for feeling pain and pleasure; with a powerful aversion from the objects producing the one, and an equally strong propensity towards those producing the other. That as he is an agent free to act or to abstain from acting, so is he responsible for the use he shall make of that freedom. That the power of conscience within him, aided by the energy of reason, can obtain him a sufficient rule by which to guide his freedom of acting; and at the same time convinces him that his responsibility is just. And lastly

lastly, that the concurrence of this reason and this conscience, added to the universal evidence of nature and the conviction of mankind, establish this awful and eventful truth, that he is the production of a supreme almighty Power, who possesses an unlimited *right* over him, and to whom he is correspondently bound by the most unlimited *obligation*; from whom he derives, together with his being, every attribute essential to his well-being; to whom his responsibility is due; and to whom it must inevitably be discharged, as soon as the short and temporary mode of his present being shall be altered.

In applying now the notion of right, which has been already defined, to the nature of man, which is here described, the question of the rights of man assumes an aspect widely different from that which it wears in the tribunes of sedition. We discover it to be an inquiry of the most solemn and sacred nature; and we find, that far from having any tendency to excite the bad and malignant passions of the heart, or to call into action the dishonest artifices of the understanding, our minds and hearts become awed in the presence of the Supreme Cause to which we find we have ascended. And that which we set out in quest of as an object of personal interest only, or of positive claim,

claim, proves upon discovery to be a question of the designs of Providence and of religious reserve.

If now it be asked, whether any right appears to be annexed to man? we can only say, that no such relation *immediately* appears on the character of man; that the most prominent and governing feature in that character is, his moral obligation, flowing from the absolute and sovereign right of his creator; and that it is only by prosecuting the inquiry, that we can ascertain whether, or not, the relation of right really appertains to him.

We have seen that *right* signifies *title*; that every right or title is ultimately derived from God. We have also seen, that man is a responsible agent, created by, and responsible to, God. If then we will allow ourselves to consider what *right in man* would signify, it will appear that it must signify, *a title devolved by God on a being, who is at the same time responsible to Him for all his conduct.*

The first thing that this presents to our notice is, that man possessing such a title, would stand in respect to God under two relations; as the object of his bounty, and as the subject of his will; as deriving a privilege from God, and as being bound under a certain obligation to God. But it it requires no great powers of discernment to perceive, that of these two relations, of being bound by certain conditions, or enriched by certain donations, there is a difference in order and priority. The plans of God are the occasion of the former; the satisfaction of man would be the end of the latter. As much as the purposes of God are of more importance in the system of the universe than the purposes of man; as much as the discharge of duty in man is of more consequence to the scheme of the creation than his enjoyment of a privilege; so much the obligation of man must transcend every other relation in him. We can indeed, in speculation, consider man as existing without the relation of right at all; but it is absolutely impossible to suppose him existing without moral responsibility, which is the very essence of his being, and without which he would belong to another order of beings, and no longer to the sphere of man. To employ a rational agent, to give him being, and to prescribe for him a sphere of acting to which responsibility should be annexed, was a determination of the divine will; it was necessary to the execution of the divine plan; but to accompany that being with circumstances of pleasure and enjoyment, which only can induce him to allege *a right*, must be an act of the divine goodness. Thus, the purpose of the divine will leads the way, and is the origin of our duty; the purpose of the divine benignity is consecutive, and can be the only possible foundation of our right. Responsibility in man, therefore, must be antecedent to every possible title in man, because responsibility is the evidence of the title of sovereignty in God. "We obey the laws of God—because they are His "will, whose right to obedience is prior to any "other consideration."* Whose right is universal, producing correspondently an universal obligation to obedience. Now, if God's "right is prior to any other consideration," and if our obligation to obedience is the first and immediate result of that right in regard of man, being in a manner commensurate with it, or at least inseparable from it, it will follow that our obligation precedes our right, as much as God's right precedes it, with which our obligation or duty, is in a manner commensurate. Our obligation therefore is also "prior to *any* other consideration"; prior of course, to any consideration of privilege or enjoyment, of which the sole purpose and end is, the gratification of our beings. All *right in man*, must therefore be subordinate to duty; for duty being the matter of responsibility,

* Ellis's *Knowledge of Div. Things from Revel. not from Reas. or Nature. p.* 227.

and responsibility being antecedent to every right, all right in man necessarily remains subordinate to duty.

Again, the subordination of right to duty appears in this; that, if it be asked, whether A. B. possesses any right, *e. g.* to life? it is impossible to answer that general question otherwise than conditionally, by expressing that he has a right to life, *provided* he has done nothing to forfeit the right. But if it be asked generally, whether A. B. is obliged to the performance of duty, or bound to obedience, the question is answered absolutely and without hesitation in the affirmative; it being impossible for man to do any thing that can liberate him from the obligation to duty with which he is born. As then the duty that binds man can never be removed, but the right that accommodates man may at any time be forfeited; it is evident, that duty in man is of a much more absolute and adhesive nature than right.

In thus pursuing the argument of right in general, to the question of right in man, which can only be determined by the nature of man, we find the ground of argument in the possession of the question of his duty, by which it is pre-occupied;

and which must be disposed of, before we can possibly proceed farther in the inquiry after his right.

And here we may observe, that in defining the nature of right, we have only spoken of a true *positive right*; because that only can be intended by those who assert an absolute, eternal, and inherent right; and have taken no notice of the relative notion of *negative right*, to which the imperfections of human society have given rise, and which annexes no real right, but only denies a right in others to annoy the possession of any one, who occupies a property to which no positive right is produced. But this negative right is in itself no right, but a simple possession, secured for a time by the negation of any right in another to disturb it. Such a right resembles that of a disseisor in the opinion of the law; " that the disseisor has only " the naked possession, because the disseisee may " enter and evect him ; but against all other persons " the disseisor has right ; and in this respect only " can be said to have the right of possession; for " in respect to the disseisee he has no right at all."* Now, to speak of a negative right in man in respect to God, who would represent the disseisee in this

* Jacob's Law Dict. *Right.*

comparison; whom man has in a manner disseised of his right of obedience; who may at any time "enter and evect him," and who will ultimately do so without fail; is what no one wearing a sound head and a sound heart, can possibly think necessary; wherefore in determining the nature of right, we have only considered a *true and positive right*; which, whether it be in any degree annexed to man, we shall endeavour to ascertain, when we have discharged the " prior consideration" of his moral obligation.

The duty of man, to which the unceasing vigilance of conscience, and the immoveable burthen of responsibility, compel his attention, is made clear to him by the instruction of his reason. By reason is meant, not that multiform conceit laid claim to by those, who are strenuous to maintain, that every man has *a right to think as he pleases*; a position groaning with absurdity, and which sufficiently discovers how incorrect the popular and colloquial notions of right are. All that can be conceded to such a proposition is, that no man has a right to control the thoughts of another. But it is of very little consequence whether any man has such a right or not, because it would be a control impossible to be exercised. The folly and fallacy of the proposition is, therefore, exposed

posed by a pious writer, by showing its impossibility. "Liberty of thought (says he) there must be in all men, good or bad, because it cannot be prevented; but the liberty of overt actions, which is the only liberty that will please libertines, there cannot be, till the laws of God lose their force, and society itself be dissolved." That man has no control over our thoughts, and that we are not responsible to man for the use we make of our thoughts, is undeniably true; but this establishes *no right to think as we please*, as the words of the proposition express. Though man has no such control, and can challenge no such responsibility, yet God has that control, and will certainly challenge that responsibility. As the acts of man proceed from the thoughts of man, the Power who obliges to a proper production of the effects, obliges also to a proper employment of the cause. If we are compelled to a particular rule of conduct by God, we are necessarily compelled to a particular employment of our minds in order to that conduct. Man can indeed control the conduct, and by that means can prevent the ill effects of irregular thinking, though he cannot control the act of thought itself. But this is not sufficient; for though " by means of hope or fear, the bad " thoughts of others may be restrained, so as to " produce no positively evil consequences, yet
the

" the same means are not adequate to render the
" thoughts in themselves good and profitable.
" So that he, whose mind is not rightly disposed,
" will at least often transgress by the omission of
" his duty*." With God, therefore, responsibility extends to thought as well as to action; because He has implanted in man a rule of wisdom uniform as Himself whom it represents; and He binds us as much to direct our thoughts towards that guide of our acting, as to adapt our acting to the instructions of that guide. By reason therefore is meant, a faculty of apprehending truth (according to the degree of evidence with which it presents itself) which is annexed to the nature of man; which perceives the obligation of man resulting from the right of the Creator; and which, when fairly and attentively directed to the evidence presented, leads the mind finally to the apprehension of the truth of revelation, and thereby to the fullest possible enlargement of the present sphere of man's moral and intellectual nature; and to the completest instruction on the subject of his duty.

---

* " Quanquam fieri possit, ut aliquis spe, metuque pravas
" cogitationes comprimat, ne noceant (quod tamen ægre fit)
" tamen non efficiet ut prosint: Itaque qui non recte animatus
" est, sæpe peccabit saltem officii omissione." Leibniz. T. iv. p. 278.

Man's duty is the over-ruling and determining circumstance of all his being; it is the rule by which he is bound to regulate his natural freedom of acting; and which directs him sometimes to obey, and sometimes to control, the propensities of his inclination. And the sum of his obligation, that score which constitutes the total of his responsibility is, the due observance, of his active and passive duties, by the guidance of reason, during the portion of time alloted him for existence.

Such is the absolute and indefeasible obligation under which man is born; which is inherent in his essence, and prior to every quality his nature may assume. The discharge of this obligation in every individual, would be the fulfilment of the will of God; the accomplishment of His design in creating man. If we suppose this design accomplished, its effect with respect to mankind would be, to render the life of every individual, free to the enjoyment of those various comforts and satisfactions, which the munificence of God has provided, and which in that event each one might, without impediment, apply to himself. In these, the faculty of enjoyment, that so sensibly shrinks from pain or molestation, would meet its natural and genuine objects. These comforts and satisfactions which are so provided, and capable of being

being so applied, on the entire discharge of duty of each, reason infers were designed to that end by their Author, who is at the same time the object of obligation and responsibility. That they were apportioned for the use of each on the event of that discharge of duty; and as all that any one can do towards obtaining them is, to discharge the sum of his own duties, he asserts it to be unjust that others, by their breach of duty, should prevent his enjoyment of that, to which he has himself complied with the condition required. He protests against the wrong, and alleges *a right*, on the ground of the determining purpose of God, discoverable by human reason.

The sum of man's duty is the will of God in what respects man; the performance of that duty is the execution of the will of God; the consequence of that performance must necessarily establish the happiness of all; the happiness of all is therefore the practical result of the fulfillment of the Divine Will. But it is also the result intended; inasmuch as he who wills the cause, wills also the effect, and the effect of obedience in each, is the establishment of happiness in all. They then who, having on their parts, discharged the duty assigned them, would apply to themselves the benefits resulting from that discharge; but find themselves unable to do so from an obstruction raised by the transgression, or neglect, of duty in others, and who are therefore frustrated of that result, designed in the scheme of God, but counteracted by the agency of man; are sensible, that such an issue is unjust, and contrary to that reason, by which only we become sensible of the will of God. They are convinced, that it is contrary to the rules by which God has constituted the human nature, and to the end for which he had designed it; that it is the inversion of the order proposed; that it was proposed, that every one should accomplish the purpose for which he was created, by discharging his duty, and that every one should, by that infallible operation, attain to those gratifications to which it will inevitably conduct. That as it is right in respect of God, that each should fulfil the will of God; so it is right in respect of every subordinate being, that each should enjoy the satisfaction consequent on that fulfilment. That if any such being should become an obstacle to another's enjoyment of those natural advantages, he conceives that it is still right that the other should enjoy them, because it is right that duty should be fulfilled, and it is only by the transgression of duty that such an obstacle can be raised. Here, then, he discovers the will of God to have so evidently designed those satisfactions to

be

be obtained by man; (being inseparable from the accomplishment of that will;) to have connected them so essentially with the discharge of moral obligation in man, which is the complement of the sphere assigned him to fulfil; that, in respect of man, he affirms it to be just and right that he should be able to acquire, by the means prescribed by God, those satisfactions which the Divine Benignity has inwoven in the scheme of his creation; he affirms that he has *a title* to them, founded on that Benignity; and he asserts *a right* to the possession of them, whenever that possession is either invaded or prevented by the transgression of others. And thus we arrive at the evidence of the moral quality of *positive right* annexed to, and existing in, man.

But it will not follow, that because man's positive right flows only from his discharge of his duty, that therefore if any one does not discharge his duty, others acquire a right to disturb him. Though this is to a certain extent admitted by reason, and is the foundation of all penal laws among mankind, yet it will not follow, that every one individually acquires a right to annoy him, who does not discharge that duty to God which is the condition of his positive right. The moral government of the world allows of no such outlawry. A man may hold a possession, because he has a positive right of property in it; he can also hold a possession, because no one may have a positive right to dispossess him; and this is the negative right of which we have already spoken. Man holds the right he received from God, absolutely, as long as he discharges the condition of his duty: he retains it in respect to men, after it is forfeited in respect to God, until the time assigned by God arrives for withdrawing it altogether. His right in respect to God is forfeited, whenever his conduct becomes intrinsically hostile to the will that devolved the right. Every deviation from the rule of duty would, in strictness, annul the right, did not the mercy of God concede something to the weakness and infirmity of man's nature; the whole scheme of which concession is specially and perfectly revealed by the dispensation of Christianity. When then the conduct is essentially and intrinsically hostile to the will which is to prevail; the right conferred in order to be exercised conformably with that will, is virtually and necessarily forfeited, upon every principle of probability, analogy, and common sense. But as no one can annoy, or disturb, the individual whose *positive right* should be thus extinguished, without at the same time departing from the course of his own duties, and pursuing a conduct tending to forfeit his right also, (except in those cases which reason, and the interests of society have, by common consent, prescribed;) and as God has reserved to his own final judgment the sole cognizance of those transgressions whose immediate object is, not the welfare of human society, but his own absolute and almighty will; the principles of human society continue in their full force, notwithstanding those transgressions, until human society shall terminate; and then comes on the settling of the score. Then the great question of the forfeiture of right, of the use and abuse of the opportunities provided by God, come under final consideration; and the determination of the circumstances by which the being of each shall be accompanied during the residue of existence, closes every retrospect on life, and drops the curtain on the events of time.

But of what effect is this right; this denial of right in others to interrupt or bar our passage to happiness, or this allegation of right in ourselves to pursue it, if in fact such an interruption may still subsist, and if they who have performed the condition for obtaining it, can nevertheless not yet obtain it? Will it be said, that if the right is *acknowledged*, it is a sufficient ground to authorise the exertion of every energy of our nature, to remove

move the intervening obstacles, and to take possession of it? So doubtless it is, provided it be by the specific process prepared and authorised by Him who conferred the right. Otherwise, the right alleged, and on which we justify the pursuit, will become impaired, and even annulled, if the course we prescribe for the pursuit encroaches on the boundary of duty; the observance of which on our part, is the sole ground of our claim, and the transgression of which on the part of others, the only justification of our pursuit. By what means then can we acquire those advantages which God has provided, when an obstruction is raised on the part of man, without at the same time deviating from that path of conduct, which alone gives us a *positive title* to those advantages?

The object we would pursue, is one flattering to our wishes, and attractive of our inclinations. The *object* of right, *that thing* to which a right is alleged, must necessarily be something desirable, something the possession, or prospect, of which, creates a sentiment of pleasure or satisfaction; otherwise, it would not be pursued; it would be shunned, which is contrary to the notion of a right, which implies, a just and perfect reason for seeking or retaining that, which we are strongly inclined to seek or to retain; thus rendering the
gratification

gratification of our nature the *end* of our pursuit. But if we also make it the *rule* of our pursuit, if we call upon our wish or inclination to conduct us in the way, we court a guide unequal to the task; active indeed and officious; one that will undertake it without hesitation, and proceed in it without concern; but one at the same time destitute of the certainty required, and under whose direction we may presently trespass beyond the boundary of right, and thereby forfeit the claim which alone sends us on our pursuit. Inclination, or desire, is not therefore a competent guide, either to mark out to us the good things to which we are entitled, or to point out to us the channel by which those good things can best be obtained. It fixes its eye upon the objects that please it best, and the shortest mathematical line to reach them, is the course which it naturally pursues. Our appeal then lies to reason. Reason has discovered to us what those things are in general, that they are the various benefits of being and enjoyment which, by God's appointment, would remain for every one's use, if all fulfilled the complement of their duty. It infers from this, that, if it were practicable, the way to obtain these benefits would be, to obtain the performance of duty; so far at least, as the actions of

men

men can have material influence on the happiness of each other. It perceives, that it would be in vain to endeavour to produce the fruit from any other stock than that on which God has appointed it to grow; but that by cultivating that stock, the fruit will be produced in luxuriance. That all partial schemes for obtaining this end, suggested by self-interest, and executed by passion, are unproductive of the fruit designed, and annul the right on which the scheme is endeavoured to be established. Reason decides, therefore, that the mode to be pursued, in order to procure a general enjoyment of life, must be one that may produce a general performance of duty.

But how is this general performance of duty to be accomplished? God, in rendering man a free agent, withheld coercion or positive control from influencing him in action; and although his free-agency will be brought to account when his present mode of being terminates, yet in the interval of human life, God has left him in the actual liberty to act or to abstain from action; to observe the rule of action prescribed to him, or to transgress that rule. How then, considering that the general tendency of man's will is in aberration from the rule of duty, can that leading interest of human life,

life, which can only be promoted by preventing the tranfgreffion of natural duty, and enforcing its obfervance, be fecured?

In a ftate of nature, or of mankind exifting in a ftate of total difunion, which fome philofophers have amufed themfelves with imagining it, it is evident it could not. In that ftate, where the natural freedom of doing good or ill would exift without direction, regulation, or control; where the natural diverfity and inequality of characters, would operate their full effects; where the ftrong would opprefs the weak, the cunning circumvent the fimple, the boifterous overwhelm the timid, the wicked in a thoufand ways afflict the good; without any power of prevention, or mode of compenfation; in fuch a ftate, a *pofitive right* in man to advantages, formed only to be the refult of an univerfal obedience to the moral rule, would be a fpeculative, nugatory right. An object to tantalize the fancy and diftract the mind, not one to gratify or confole the heart. Such a ftate would be a chaos of obedience and tranfgreffion, a ftate of remedilefs confufion, of the moft pofitive and radical inequality of enjoyment and fecurity.

If man in a state of nature, and left in the unrestrained freedom of doing good or ill, is unable to attain to happiness; what resource is left, what means exist to help him to attain it?

We have seen that the perfect discharge of duty throughout mankind would, without further operation, establish for each those general advantages, to which our nature tends, and which, from the title, or right, we claim to them on behalf of the God of Nature, we are in the habit of expressing by the words, natural rights. If a scheme, therefore could be effected among men, that would enforce such a discharge of duty, this scheme, as far as it went, would be a contrivance to secure and perpetuate right.

Such a scheme is civil government. Man's obligation to God comprehends the total of his duty; civil government concerns itself exclusively in enforcing the discharge of that portion of duty, by which the happiness of mankind can be in any degree influenced; in order to realise that happiness, and to obtain the presence of those circumstances, which man esteems to be the objects of his *natural right*.

To say what these are, off hand as Mr. Paine has done, with so much facility and so much decision, is what no sincere and conscientious man will do. He will not doubt his ability, by the aid of inquiry, to discover them as effectually as Mr. Paine pretends to have done; and by the aid of argument, to establish them at least as solidly; but he will be thoroughly convinced, that inquiry and argument are necessary for his success.

Man's right, as well as his duty, is to be collected from the design of God who devolved it. As we have shown it to be consecutive on his duty, and subordinate to it, it follows that there cannot exist a right intrinsically hostile to, or destructive of, a duty. By our duty we are bound; " First, to the
" interests of the universe, or of God who presides
" over it; secondly, to those of the human nature;
" thirdly, to those of our particular society; by
" this subordination, in case of opposition of inte-
" rest, the will, or, if we may so speak, the utility
" of God, is to be preferred to the utility of the
" human nature; that of the human nature, to
" the utility of any particular society; and that of
" the society to which we belong, to our own pri-
" vate utility." * The privilege *conferred* by God on

* " Primum mundo, seu rectori ejus Deo, deinde generi humano,
" deinde reipublicæ: Hac subordinatione, ut in casu pugnantiæ,
voluntas,

man, can never be paramount to the duty *imposed* by God on man. Thus, man's duty being known in any one instance, there cannot exist a right, a true positive right, destructive of that duty. And if unbounded ambition, a thirst of blood, contempt for religion, indifference for the quiet and comfort of mankind, are called forth into activity, they become the transgression of the highest and most sacred portion of duty, and consequently the forfeiture of every right. Those crimes being essentially and eternally contrary to the duty of man, and never to be reconciled to it on the ruffian plea of necessity.† For, as man's best rights are subordinate to all his duties, it is possible that a duty of forbearance might direct him to abstain from the pursuit of the most alluring form of right; and they therefore who would promote the activity of those passions, under the fal-

---

" voluntas, seu utilitas Dei, si ita loqui licet, præferatur utili-
" tati generis humani, et hæc utilitati reipublicæ, et hæc pro-
" priæ." Leibniz, tom. iv. p. 185. P. II.

† ——" Should I at your harmless innocence
" Melt, as I do, yet public reason just,
" Honor and empire with revenge enlarged,
" By conqu'ring this new world, compels me now
" To do, what else, tho' damn'd, I should abhor."
---So spake the Fiend, and with *necessity*
The *tyrant's plea*, excus'd his devilish deeds.

Par. Lost IV. 389.

lacious

lacious pretext of establishing a right, involve themselves in the guilt, and of course in the forfeiture; nor can a mode be imagined for recovering the right, without returning within the precincts of duty, which constitute at the same time the boundary of right.

Many considerations, therefore, must precede a judgment given upon this question. Reason must exercise herself on certain *data*, before she can pronounce a decision, or deduce a conclusion; but least of all will she admit, without examination, and without tracing their connexion with truth, the promptings of interest and passion in their own cause; least of all will she surrender up her judicial authority, to the petulance and clamour of fancy and of error.

To specify the natural rights of man, would be to enumerate every possible advantage or satisfaction that would ensue an universal and complete discharge of duty; which surpass the calculation, as they exceed the expectation, of man. This may be considered as the extreme speculative point of man's right. A point of imaginary perfection, not more to be looked for in fact, than any other of those perfections, which it is possible for the mind to survey in contemplation, but which youth,
igno-

ignorance, or enthusiasm only, can be idle enough to expect. Short of this extreme point, however, are many degrees of practicable enjoyment of those good things we call our rights; abundantly sufficient to answer every important purpose for which man is placed on earth, and to satisfy all those inclinations, that reason will either encourage or approve. To attain these he is propelled, sometimes, by the impulse of desire, sometimes by the instigation of duty; again, to regulate or check his pursuit of them, he is sometimes constrained by the force of conscience, sometimes by the positive prohibition of duty. To specify or enumerate all the objects to which the right annexed to man has respect, would therefore be impossible, since those objects vary their relation to man according as circumstances vary, and according to the relative instructions of duty. So that what is one day the object of a right; another day loses that relation altogether. Thus, the right to life, which is alleged to be a practicable right to day, may be converted into a nugatory right to-morrow, by being cast on a desolate shore without the means of subsistence; or it may be forfeited, by the commission of crime, that is by the trangression of duty; or it may be overruled by a superior right, as when duty, which is the right of God, directs to surrender it; or it may be simply withdrawn, as it effectually is, when

man

man is removed from the present scene of existence. And this is sufficient to show us, how incorrect the notions of right, promulgated by the professed heralds of the Rights of Man, are; with what inconsiderate haste their equivocal nomenclature has been adopted; and what a tangle of thoughts and conceits this hasty adoption must unavoidably produce.

But, if it exceeds the possibility of human calculation to ascertain all "*those good things which God has provided*" to be the result of universal obedience, it may perhaps be possible to adduce such of them as are of principal use and accommodation; such as the human nature demands for the perfection of its different powers; we may be able to form some notion of that condition of being which would follow such obedience, and use it as a general rule in delineating what we conceive to be, our natural rights, or, the genuine objects of that right or title which we affirm to have been annexed to us, by the bounty of the God of Nature.

And this we cannot better do, than by letting ourselves inquire, without fastidiousness or fear, *Why* man is favoured with any such privilege at all? This question it cannot be difficult to resolve; for, as the privilege is conferred by infinite wisdom,

dom, the reason of man will most probably be able to trace out some motive or final cause, in respect of which it is conferred. And this will at the same time greatly contribute to determine, the nature and extent of the privilege itself. In a general view, those objects are certain circumstances necessary to the well-being of man, and constituting the best condition of his present nature; and the presence of which, produces a sentiment of complacency and satisfaction in him; the question then is, Why is man endowed with the means of obtaining the presence of those circumstances, and why does their presence produce a pleasurable sentiment in him?

It is the natural effect of the continued action of the force of habit, to obtund and deaden our observing and sentimental faculties, even against objects the best adapted to excite them; but if we can suppose ourselves suddenly brought into being, possessing all those faculties in their full perfection and vivacity, because unimpaired by custom, the visible objects of nature would rouse in us that sentiment which Milton so beautifully ascribes to Eve:

" That day I oft remember, when from sleep
" I first awak'd, and found myself repos'd
" Under a shade on flow'rs, *much wondering whence,*
" *And what I was, whence thither brought, and how.*"

If we claim then the character of philosophers, (and such is the universal ambition of the age) let us awaken this reasonable surprise, which forty or fifty years are not qualified to extinguish; and let us not wear our existence like children, who never asked themselves that pregnant question,

———" What am I, and from whence?"

Let us not shrink from an inquiry so aidful to the present argument. Why is man formed with the power of applying to himself those advantages of outward circumstance, by which the faculties of his nature are fostered and brought to their best maturity, and which he calls his natural rights? The answer is obvious and conclusive. It is, in order that he may, without control or hindrance, execute the task for which he is placed on earth, and for the performance of which he is accountable; and the sentiment of pleasure is annexed, primarily, as a stimulant to urge him to pursue the situation in which his powers may be best qualified for the discharge of his duty; secondarily, as a provision of bounty, to render his inevitable existence a circumstance of delight. For that his existence, in respect of himself, is inevitable, appears from this; that it depended in no degree upon his own consent, but upon the absolute will of Him whose purpose it suited to employ him in the scheme of His creation; and from this also, that let him strain and struggle as he will, he can never detach from himself the growing burthen of responsibility, until it be finally removed by the same terrific and almighty hand that first attached it.

The end of this privilege, then, appears to be, first, to enable man to possess his being free for obedience to the will of God; and secondly, to render that being happy and delightful to himself. But the first of those purposes is, in every respect, anterior to the latter. Man knows the duty to which he himself is obliged, and in knowing this, he knows the rule by which every other man is obliged. The observation of this rule is the sum of each man's obligation, the measure of his responsibility; and from that observance flows the positive right he derives to those things, which, unhappily for precision, he has also chosen to call his rights. To observe this rule is to pursue the course that leads to the right to, and to the possession of, happiness. To pursue that right and that possession by the only course prescribed by God, would be to discharge the complement of our duty, and to fulfil the end of our being. Here, then, is an intimacy which nothing can dissolve, a relation which nothing can disturb. He that will discharge the condition of his nature, will establish a positive right; he that would acquire a positive right, must discharge the condition of his nature.

The negative right above spoken of, which, as we observed, is in fact no right, but only actual possession secured for a short time by the non-existence of any human right to invade it, may satisfy those who terminate their views and speculations in this narrow and sordid sphere of being; it may, for the present, answer every end of ambition, of plunder, of cruelty, of revenge, of oppression, but it will never, even here, be able to supply the place of that true, positive right, designed by God's goodness, in the mind of any one who is conscious of the nature he wears; who values happiness only according to its permanency; and who has accustomed his reason and his sentiment to swell to the extent of that duration, which all the efforts of impiety and wickedness cannot abridge; and to which they who shun it, equally as they who court it, will at last be obliged to submit.

As each one is bound to the condition of duty, each, while he discharges his own duty, may resist any interruption he might experience from another's deviation from the course of his duty. He can do this upon two grounds; first, because such an interruption may not only obstruct his personal gratitification, which is a secondary consideration, but it may also obstruct the service in which he is employed by God, which is his principal concern; secondly, because the satisfactions which are provided to be the result of universal obedience, can only be obtained by that obedience, and each can only contribute the sum of his own obedience. So that he is *obliged* to resist the interruptions he might experience in the discharge of his duty, by the transgression of duty in others, unless when the rule of obligation prohibits the resistance; and he is *authorised* to exercise the right his obedience has given him, in obtaining what the transgression of others deprive him of, by compelling that obedience which only can procure it.

Here, then, man is directed by duty, to employ active means for controlling the transgression of others, whenever it interferes with the discharge of his duty, in all cases where that duty does not enjoin submission; and he is privileged by right, to employ active means of acquiring for himself those advantages, which the transgression of others only can withhold from him, unless where the same duty enjoins forbearance; so that, in both cases, the regulation of man's conduct remains ever and equally under the absolute control and direction of duty.

All

All this, however, in the way of *fact*, man *can* do, and apply all these benefits to his own use, even though he have forfeited his positive *right*, provided he has not transgressed in those particulars which entitle society to abridge him of that capacity. For, as God has reserved the cognizance of these cases entirely to himself, and has not left to us the liberty " of judging of another man's " servant;" as long as life continues, every such person can assume the benefits due only to obedience, on the same principle as the " *sun is made* " *to rise* equally *upon the just and the unjust* ;" and he may challenge the duty of others, equally as if he discharged that condition which alone can give him a true title so to do. He may thus pass the residue of his life in abuse of the regulations of God; a sort of privileged usurper; but the advantage, if any it is, can be but of very short continuance, and is obtained at the dreadful price of an insolvent responsibility. But these being infractions of, and therefore exceptions from, the general plan, they of course form no part of that statement, in which our only aim is to establish the truth.

The right use of the power and faculties of man, is the object of duty; these powers and faculties are confided to his care; and he is not only to use them

them well on every distinct occasion, but in general, to maintain them in the best condition attainable. If the departure from duty in others goes to invade those powers or faculties, we must resist and repel the invasion; in doing which, we discharge a duty; but at the same time, in consequence of an union established by the divine goodness, we acquire a gratification. The discharge of the duty however is the first in order, as it is in importance. If we made the latter our first motive, we should have no certain rule by which to act; for gratification is to be found in innumerable objects, entirely distinct from, often directly contrary to, our duty. We should presently exceed our right, and lose it instead of confirming it. When duty ceases to direct us to such resistance, prudence commands us to halt; we have lost our only infallible guide; personal satisfaction is the only candidate to succeed her; and the vicinity of error cautions us not to hazard an advance, lest we find ourselves in rapid progress beyond the line of duty, and risk to sacrifice the right for which only we contend. As the will of God is what most concerns a moral and responsible creature; and as, when that will is satisfied, the principal concern of man is satisfied, we may reasonably remain contented with the satisfactions which an unrestrained power of discharging our obligations to God will afford; especially

cially as the bounty of God has so enriched the world with means of enjoyment, adapted to every situation in it; and as even the practicable degrees of obedience attainable amongst men, furnish every thing that man's nature can absolutely need, or reasonably desire.

The rule of duty, as it is the general rule provided in nature, so it is, at the same time, the most distinct and satisfactory one for ascertaining what our nature absolutely demands. When we are conscious that the discharge of a duty is required of us, and that it is within our power to remove the impediment that obstructs us in the discharge of it, then the removing the impediment incorporates itself into the duty to be discharged, and becomes a part of it. If it be our duty to repel an intrusion, by repelling it we discharge a duty. If the intrusion be at the same time, afflictive of our feelings, as well as obstructive of our duty; if the removal of it procures us those benefits we call our rights, as well as enable us to discharge those obligations we call our duties; in pursuing the right we discharge a duty, in discharging the duty, we establish a right. Such is the indissoluble union, established by the goodness of the Creator, between natural duty and right in man; between that absolute and indefeasible
obliga-

obligation under which man is born, and that original and comprehensive right annexed to his nature by its Author, which our adversaries, if they mean any thing, must be supposed to mean, by " *abso-lute right*." " Those absolute rights which are vested in him by the immutable laws of nature," and which, " such as are social and relative result from, and are posterior to. Those absolute rights, which are usually summed up in one general appellation, and denominated the natural liberty of mankind—being a right inherent in us by birth, and one of *the gifts of God to man* at his creation.*" " This is the *only true and solid foundation* of man's dominion over external things, whatever airy metaphysical notions may have been started by fanciful writers upon this subject.†"

Man is not to quarrel for his rights, like children for their cakes or toys; as if the whole purpose and end of them was to gratify his individual propensities. The end and purpose of right in man, or of the moral power of acquiring those outward circumstances which have been called his absolute rights, is, to render his being as perfect as it will admit of. But for why? Not primarily for the

* Blackstone's Comm. b. i. p. 124—5. † Ib. b. ii. p. 3.

plea-

pleasure, amusement, or indulgence of man. No one who has ever reflected upon Infinite Wisdom, can hold so coarse and sottish a belief. But it is, to render him a more free and efficient agent within his department, to execute the purpose of God. It is, that he may be under the best circumstances for accomplishing the design of Infinite Wisdom in the sphere prescribed for him, and with which his real happiness is indissolubly linked. In proportion as the actual situation of man is destitute of those circumstances, or removed from that perfection; and that he feels himself unable to pursue the course that he is conscious is prescribed to him, without exercising his active powers in overcoming impediments obstructing that course; in the same proportion the efforts he makes to emancipate himself from these constraints, become the discharge of that duty, which, as it requires a good employment of his powers, requires necessarily the maintenance of those powers in the best and the most free condition attainable. On the other hand, in proportion as he possesses these favourable circumstances, and approaches to that perfection, the necessity of such efforts diminishes, and the right remaining to be secured is reduced. But if at any time he is so invested with the circumstances required for his well-being, and approximates so nearly to that perfection, as to possess the full and free agency of his responsible faculties; to be able to expand his nature to the widest capacity of the sphere in which his creator has placed him, and to discharge his duty without molestation or constraint; then, the duty of self-emancipation ceases with the occasion for it, and of course all the right, which cannot outlast the occasion. And every degree of violence employed, every interruption of general tranquillity produced, with a view only to promote the interest of personal ambition, or to obtrude the speculations of enthusiasm, under the pretext of ascertaining a natural right, being deserted of the only ground of reason that could give it support as such, becomes an unqualified and bare transgression of duty; and is a crime aggravated in its nature, in as much as it has the audacity to plead *a natural right*, which signifies a *title*, or *grant*, conferred by God, at the very time that it is openly and impiously transgressing his commands.

How this may apply to England, we leave it with YOU to determine. Look back to the past histories of mankind. Look forth upon the present face of human affairs. Look to the principles of that Constitution which, till the French eruption, we were all taught to revere; and to the practical blessings flowing from it, which we still do not cease to enjoy; and then do YOU pronounce, whether *this* is the country, in which the nature of man is destitute of the circumstances, that enable him to execute freely the great purpose for which he was placed on earth; whether *this* is the country, in which man's nature may not attain to the greatest degree of perfection, (consequently of natural happiness,) attainable by man? And if this is not the case; if the contrary should prove to be the case; if the annals of our distinguished nation, the biography of our illustrious countrymen, our own unvarying experience, and the concurring sentiments of every rival people, exclaim against the ingratitude and blasphemy of such a doubt; then, neither is it the country in which ambitious violence, or turbulent intrigue, can escape the abhorrence of the reasonable and virtuous portion of mankind; the curses of a neglected and defrauded posterity; and, what is far worse, the fullest measure of condemnation, at the future tribunal of heaven.

What has been stated, shows the nature, origin, and end of natural right in man. It is communicated from God, who has annexed it to our nature; and made it dependent on the fulfilment of that obligation, by which we are bound, antecedently to any annexation of right. In annexing a right to our nature, God assigns over to each of us an interest in that general obligation, by which all are bound to Him. For as right and obligation are reciprocal, (all right necessarily producing a correspondent obligation) and as the obligation by which man is bound in duty to man, is no other than a part of the obligation by which all are bound in obedience to the will of God; it is clear, that the right which man is enabled to claim in respect of man, and which produces a corresponding obligation, can be no other than the sovereign right of God, partially and conditionally communicated by Him to man. The notion of right in man, therefore, springs from a notion of obedience, or, of duty discharged on his part. Its genuine objects can only be obtained, by an universal discharge of duty. To produce this general discharge of duty, (at least in such respects as influence in the intercourse between man and man) as the only practicable method for obtaining those objects, is the design of civil government; which is employed, in contriving the means for producing that conduct from whence the general good may result, and in putting those means into execution.

Duty, therefore is the *rule* by which civil government acts, in order to attain the *end* for which it was devised, namely, the happiness of mankind, during

their

their transient existence upon earth. That it has been so considered by the best and wisest of men, from the first dawn of civil polity, to its full meridian in Britain, might be showed by an host of evidence. But such evidence would contribute nothing towards determining the present controversy, in which a formal appeal is made from the collective energies of reason, and her most applauded decisions in time past, to the collusive assertions, and canvassed assents, of the interest and passion of the day. We therefore wave the venerable support we might bring to the argument from that evidence, and content ourselves with showing, that without reference to times past, or to any extraneous authority whatever, if they will only consent to let reason at the present day be arbitrator in the dispute, she will decide and demonstrate to the fullest conviction, that duty is the only possible rule or basis of civil government; and that no positive *right in man* can be deduced, or imagined, that has not its origin in a notion of duty.

If we would, in a few words, expose the reason of that prodigious difference which appears between the system of society propagated from the French eruption, and every other that the practice of mankind had before experienced, or the ingenuity of philosophers devised, it perhaps could not be

more

more clearly done than by saying, that every other system of government, every other form of social union, every discourse on human law, every treatise on jurisprudence, has laid its first foundation in, *the duty of man.** They have conceived it to be the natural and necessary source of every good that law, government, or society, can possibly intend; the only rule by which it can be obtained. France, on the other hand, labours to make *right,* or, as they equivocally call it, the *the rights of man,* the basis and rule of all government. To their arbitrary, uncertain, and fluctuating notions of this right, they endeavour to square and bend the nature of duty; instead of using the distinct, unalterable, and only unerring rule of duty, to trace out the natural form and real proportions of right. When we consider this new system, in comparison with what the world had conceived before that instructress opened her school, we appear to see two cones, the one inverted and labouring to erect itself upon its apex, the other standing on its broad foundation, and established without effort by the immutable laws of nature.

---

* " Rationi valde consentaneum existimem, politicas institu-
" tiones *exordiri* ab illa prima philosophiæ moralis parte, quæ,
" velut unica vitæ hominum rectrix et magistra, *singulos sui*
" *muneris ac officii admonet.*" Bibliogr. Politica Naudæi. Grotii. Diss. 12mo.

When Plato considered the effects of civil government, and the benefit that it was enabled to impart to mankind by restraining crime and compelling to duty, his admiration drew from him the doubt, whether it were not a scheme of divine original, a contrivance communicated from God * to man. Though Plato may be derided, or forgotten, in France, though he may be without authority in England, yet every feeling and thinking person will recognise the ground of his admiration, and will discern, that if civil government was not formally communicated from God, it necessarily arose out of the provisions of God, the relations of man, and the instructions of reason. It had one general end, common to every local situation of man, namely, the acquirement and security of those advantages which can only be withheld from the obedient by the transgression of the disobedient; and it employed one universal mean to attain its end, namely the coercion of crime, and the compulsion to duty.

These advantages, common to every situation of man, because adapted to the common nature, constitute the natural object which the right annexed to man respects. These, by abuse of language, are in common phrase called, the natural rights of

---

* Θεος ἢ τις ἀνθρωπων ὑμιν, ὦ ξενοι, εἴληφε την αἰτιαν της των νομων διαθεσεως; Κ Λ. Θεος, ὦ ξενε, θεος· ὡς γε το δικαιοτατον ἐιπειν.   *De legibus.* I.

man; from being the appropriate object of the right annexed to his particular nature, by the Author of universal nature.

In attempting to ascertain what these are, it is of the highest importance to be careful to distinguish, between the instructions of reason, and the promptings of passion. As the objects that can induce man to assert a right, must possess allurements to intice him to pursue them, and as every object that flatters or pleases the passions, possesses strong allurements also, it is of extreme consequence to discriminate, between the consent of reason, and the propensity of inclination; between those allurements, towards which reason favours the propensity, and those, towards which the propensity is wholly urged by the activity of passion; lest by mistaking the one for the other, endless confusion and misadventure should ensue. To endeavour, therefore, to ascertain the proper object of a right annexed to man, solely by the quality of the temptations they may present; that is, by the relation they shall bear to our inclinations and our wishes, and not to that fundamental reason which alone establishes the right to them, would at the best be equivocal; and would furnish us with no substantial evidence that our inquiries had been successful. It would be inclination appealing to its own verdict; there would neither be authority nor proof. Such a process cefs might advance the interests of anarchy or sedition, but would be radically destructive of the interests of civil government.

If truth is the object (and we are to suppose it to be so till we have either proof, or *very shrewd reasons to suspect* that it is not) we must look for some test by means of which that truth may be tried. Of the validity of this test reason is to judge; but reason discovers no such validity in the plea set up by inclination or desire, unsupported by other authority. Where then can we look for such a test? we have seen how intimate an union subsists between duty and right in man; that they, in a manner, shape each other's course; that they confine on each other's territory, that the outline of duty, becomes at the same time the delineation of right. From the well-examined country of duty, we are to proceed in quest of discoveries, in the unexplored, or uncertain district of right. The duty of man we know; with this given quantity it will not be difficult to obtain the produce of right. It is a rule that cannot mislead us. It offers nothing to allure our passions; it comprehends nothing to bias our judgment, but rather to rouse it to a scrutinising jealousy. Right, on the contrary, presents nothing but allurement, nothing but personal satisfaction. In the inquiry after duty therefore, our selfish passions are at rest, and the energy of reason is employed, without importunity or hindrance, in determining its claim.

The duty of man has different immediate objects; in relation to these, moralists have classed, his duty to God, his duty to his fellow, and his duty to himself. The rule of these duties is apprehended by his reason in different degrees of evidence and perspicuity, according as it collects it, either from the effort of private reflection; or, from the united energies of man, unaided by superior light; or from the communication of truth from the source, imparting to man a thorough and complete knowledge of his own nature, and of the sovereign will, which is the only ultimate rule of human acion. In whichever of these degrees of evidence man is able to acquire the knowledge of that will, whether it be from the law of nature, or from that of revelation, the most perspicuous and comprehensive within his power to obtain constitutes the rule of his several duties; all of which compose the sum of his obligation, the measure of the service for which he was placed on earth. To instigate to the discharge of these duties, God placed in us conscience, which propells to this discharge, according to the degree of exercise it has received; and he has annexed to

their

their discharge certain enjoyments, congenial to our natures, which allure us to discharge them. Thus wisely providing both for the first impulse towards duty, and for its final accomplishment. So that to effect the purpose of God, and to procure the happiness of man, requires the same process.*

To obtain this double end, to promote the service of God, and the consequent happiness of man, the Creator laid in him those principles, which immediately produced the fruit of society ripening into government. They anticipated the wild inequality of nature, and confirmed each on the same just level of individual security. Those whose

---

* It is on this account that pious writers are apt to inculcate, that the happiness of man is *the end* of God in creating him. That it is *an end* of his creation, we have the fullest and most affecting evidence; we perceive that it is an inevitable consequence of the accomplishment of the divine will; that it is therefore a part of the divine purpose. But, to say therefore that it is, exclusively, *the end* of his being, is what we are not authorised to pronounce. It is enough for us, that it is a necessary consequence of the execution of the divine plan in the creation of man. But as it may be only a partial and collateral consequence; and as there may be other designs within the scope of Infinite Wisdom, in introducing the moral agent man into the universe; it may be a source of error, and an occasion of presumption, to assert that the happiness of man was *the sole end* of his being; and it answers every moral purpose, for man to be well aware, that extreme and eternal happiness is *an unavoidable result* of his conforming with the rules prescribed for his acting by the sovereign will.

excess of force would have induced them to molest the common pursuit of happiness, were abridged of their injurious vigour, and reduced to the general level that the rule of duty prescribed. Those whom natural weakness or timidity withheld from the benefits they might rightfully have assumed, were invigorated from the collective strength of the union, and raised to the same level of secure existence.

How that collective strength was first produced; how government gained its original ascendency; and how the rebellious will of man that government is established to control, so far controlled itself at first, as to submit to the constraint of government, has been a matter of just astonishment in every age of wise research. Certainly it never happened as some theorists have assumed; that men, actuated by a general impulse of wisdom, met to concert a regular compact of union, or form of subordination. The very essence of government; which is, *coercion*;* and its object, which is, *man*

---

* " The design of polical society is, to secure the tranquillity
" of all its members. In order to this, it was necessary to take
" measures for suppressing all attempts to disturb the public
" peace. Experience has discovered, that the support of society
" depends entirely on the *coercive power*, which by exemplary
" punishments intimidates the wicked, and balances the allure-
" ments of pleasure, and the strength of the passions." Goguet.
Origin of Laws, &c. V. 1. p. 19.

himself

himself; render this conjecture inadmissible. The growth of government can be traced with much fairer internal evidence of probability, on the scriptural foundation, by supposing mankind to have spread out from one original family, instructed by the Author of their reason, and extending patriarchal authority, till it became supplanted by some other more comprehensive.

Such was the general nature, design, and end, of social regulation. But the extent of the habitable earth, the prodigious numbers of the human race, and the influence of various concurring causes, occasioned man to form different and distinct societies. A scheme of government comprehending all, would have been in various respects impracticable and unnecessary; wherefore mankind, being divided by the progress of events, and by other incidental causes, into different associations, each of these exerted itself to accomplish that scheme, which was to be productive of so much benefit to all. But hence arose various diversities in the modes which each devised, while they provided their respective regulations, established their particular customs, and constituted the artificial organs by which wisdom was to direct, and power act, for the welfare of the whole. These modes being differently influenced in different

societies

societies, by partial and local circumstances, or by peculiar occurrences, induced different characters of states; resembling each other necessarily in this only, that they sought the same general end, by the same general means; but at the same time, and under the control of that general principle, they admitted various distinct, and subordinate principles for their respective societies; arising from climate, soil, extent, and other relative considerations. The first, and governing principle, respected man's absolute nature; the second, and subordinate principle, respected man's relative situation. Here was a great field for the characters, passions, vices, virtues, and talents of men to display themselves; each of which more or less aided to influence the circumstances of every particular society. In some, the great original purpose of government was better executed than in others. Some exhibited more, and some less skill. In some, the passions were more, in others less, restrained. In some, the energies of the mind, the foundations of moral duty, the arts of life, the principles of science, were more, in others less, cultivated. In all, two rules were professed or implied; namely, first, the general rule in respect of which government was *originally* established; secondly, the particular rule according to which the particular society was *actually* arranged. The first comprehended
those

thofe general interefts of man's nature, which it is effential for him to fecure; the fecond included thofe particular interefts of man's fituation, which it is highly convenient for him to poffefs. The firft of thefe form what are intended by the phrafe, *natural rights*; the fecond, what are intended by the name of *civil* or *municipal rights*. The rule of the former is the abfolute will of God, obfcurely adumbrated by the law of nature, but accurately defined by the law of revelation; the rule of the latter is the notorious practice of the fociety, diftinctly expofed by the evidence of enacted laws, and immemorial ufage. If the laws and cuftoms of a fociety, comply with the will of God in what refpects the natural duty of man, by binding each one, without refpect or favour, to the obfervance of that duty, which all muft obferve in order that each may be enfured of enjoying his natural right; they are at full liberty to eftablifh their forms, as circumftances fhall direct; nor can any reafonable appeal be made from the varieties of fuch a government, to any rule whatever of natural right, which refufes to take cognizance of all fuch matters. As long as fuch a fociety continues not to infringe upon that facred object, natural right is fatisfied. The wifdom of fucceeding generations under fuch a government, being exercifed on matters within its own experience, the accumulation of their

labours

labours constitutes the most secure and solid basis upon which civil society can possibly rest. Nor can any call for internal change, in such a government be urged, upon a plea of natural right; all the claims of which are fully satisfied, whenever all are equally constrained by the operation of the force of law. And if, of two societies, in each of which this great object should be *secured*, the one should exist a republic and the other a monarchy, it would be a crime of the same specific quality for a party to endeavour, to erect the former into a monarchy, as to depress the latter into a republic; because in both cases it would be an offence against the fundamental law of the polity; which, when the claims of natural duty and natural right are satisfied, constitutes the highest authority to which, under God, man is obliged to submit. If on principles agreeable to wisdom, and by means consistent with duty, the society were to produce that change, there would be no blame, there would even be a right; but it is not the desire of forty or fifty leaders, of six or seven clubs, of eight or ten thousand mutineers, that can constitute a sufficient and reasonable ground for disturbing a system under which eight millions of individuals live in the security of their lives and liberties; in the practical enjoyment of every object to which the Creator has conveyed, them a right; and in the unmolested profits of their labour, ingenuity, or industry.

To fix the boundary of natural right, to say what every man *may* do, we must look to the rule we have so repeatedly enforced, and say what every man *must* do; we must look to duty, and by its aid delineate right. We must look to the duty required of him who would exercise a right, and to the duty required of him who would invade or impede that exercise; for if all perform their duty, that is, if each does his own duty, so that no one annoys or molests another, each is virtually in possession of every object to which he has a right, the bounty and providence of God having disposed the objects to which he has communicated a right, within the reach of human industry.

We are told in an authoritative tone, that man's natural rights are *life, liberty,* and *equality*: To any fair reasoner we would grant this position, because such an one would not make a swindling use of the concession, but would take care that the terms he used should be uniform in their meaning, and defined in their extent. We would grant the position upon this fair ground, that man has a *right* to retain his *life,* as long as it pleases God he should do so; that he has a *right* to a *free* use of those natural faculties for the exercise of which life was given him; and that *all men* have *equally* a *right* to those benefits. But it is impossible to make this concession to the antagonists who stand opposite to us in the controversy, without burthening it with tedious limitations; because the same equivocation that we have perceived to exist in their word *right*, extends itself to every word in their vocabulary.

That we may not, however, appear to decline the question under any form, and thereby virtually to concede that which we altogether refuse, let us endeavour to discover in what way man can claim a right to such things as are conveyed to the understanding by the words, *life*, *liberty*, and *equality*. Man is created by God, and endowed with reason; a sphere of action is assigned him, and he is rendered severely accountable for his use of it. He is thus placed in life first of all for that end, and his *life* is the first circumstance necessary for accomplishing it; since, by extinguishing *the life*, the whole agency is at once destroyed, and the purpose entirely defeated. That man should *live*, was therefore God's will; and destroying the life, in its first effect, is counteracting the will of God. There is no great mystery in the right to life; if man is to perform a service, he must *live* in order to do so. As life is rendered, by God's goodness, an object of desire, as well as of obligation, man adheres to it independently of duty;

duty; but still, as the means of defending it are confided to him, he is to maintain it as the *substratum* of the agency vested in him. But he has also a distinct and personal interest in retaining life; it was given him, first for use, and next for enjoyment; the second consequence of impairing life is, impairing the rightful interest of man. Man resigns up his life to the Donor without conceiving the notion of a *right* to retain it; but if any but the Donor threatens to disturb it, unless it be in evident conformity with the will of the Donor, the notion of a duty to defend it, and of a right to preserve it, suggest themselves to his mind. The former, as he looks to God, to whom he is accountable for it; the latter, as he looks to his adversary, who has no authority to disturb it. Man *must* live to be able to fulfil the sphere assigned him, till God dispense with the necessity; man *may* live, and avail himself of that permission in the most effectual manner (provided he does not attempt to satisfy his personal inclination by means adverse to the will of God) until God withdraw the permission. Man's life, on a general aspect, presents itself to our thoughts in no other way than as a matter of fact. In respect of any unjust attempt from man to impair it, it may be alleged an object of right holden of God; but even then its defence is no less a matter of duty also. And though we may defend it with greater alacrity on the ground of right, as feeling the urgency of personal interest, yet we are called upon to defend it on the ground of duty also, until duty forbid us to defend it, and then surely the right to defend it ceases altogether. Such appears to be the nature of the *right to life*, as far as we can render it intelligible to our understanding.

The right to *liberty*, seems to flow necessarily from the right to *life* just explained. For, as it is necessary *to live*, in order to *hold* the agency assigned to us; so, in order to *execute* that agency by the rule prescribed, it is necessary to be *free* to do so; that is, that our beings and faculties should be free from all unreasonable and vexatious constraint, embarrassing or impeding the execution of our office. If we suppose the rule of duty faithfully and universally observed, and duty discharged on all parts, every man will have acted without the hindrance or impediment of others; this is the *first degree* of freedom to which we are entitled, because it is inseparable from the actual discharge of the duty to which we are obliged. But, as every man's activity, who directs it by the rule of duty, is sufficiently controled, the residue of liberty that remains after the discharge of duty, being unproductive of evil, forms the *second degree*

of

of that freedom, which man, by God's bounty, is entitled to enjoy.

These form the sum total of the benefits sought for in the scheme of civil government, and are therefore comprehensive of every other. They establish the liberty of acting; and of course, all the natural consequences of acting; the whole of which may be included under the notion of *property*; which " consists in a free use, enjoyment, " and disposal of all the acquisitions without any control or diminution, (save only by the laws of the land,")* that man renders the objects of his acting; whatever be the mode, or quality, of those acquisitions; whether corporeal or mental, whether they be of wealth, or reputation. This freedom of action is of two sorts or degrees; first, freedom to proceed without restraint in the course prescribed by God; secondly, freedom to assume every personal satisfaction to which that course naturally conducts. As duty is anterior to right, and as the performance of duty not only leads in its issue to certain enjoyments, but is also ever necessarily accompanied in its progress with certain other enjoyments, (the circumstances that enable us best to fulfil our duties, being such as are at

* Blackstone's Comm. B. I. p. 138.

the same time most satisfactory to our natures; it follows, that the enjoyments which are coeval with duty, and inseparable from it, must be anterior to those which are consequent on duty; and that they therefore constitute the first and most prominent part of our natural satisfactions, or, to use the popular phrase, of our natural rights. That freedom which we enjoy, when we freely discharge our obligation to God, constitutes much the most considerable and momentous portion of our freedom, since it secures to us the free use of our life, of our persons, of our natural and intellectual powers, and of the means of maintaining and improving them all; and is therefore productive of all our highest enjoyments. These enjoyments from freedom, which are inseparable from the free discharge of our indefeasible obligation to God, we can virtually define, by defining the duty with which they are commensurate. It is our duty, to make the best use of the faculties committed to us, in conformity with the rule prescribed to our intelligence; it is therefore our duty to maintain our faculties in the best condition; since it is all one to use our faculties ill ourselves, or to allow of their detereoration by causes within our power to control. We are therefore to resist every counteracting cause, that would impair the faculties that we are obliged to bring to a good fruit.

If

If we have gained that degree of freedom which empowers us to accomplish this great end; if our condition be such as to enable us to obtain full knowledge of the purposes of God, of the permanent interests of man, and of the measure of his responsibility, and at the same time freely to act according to all this knowledge; if our *lives* are secure, our persons *free*, and that the faculties of the mind and heart are provided with an opportunity of expanding to the widest capacity of their nature; if no impediment or obstruction is offered to this growth, no unnatural constraint tending to dwarf or distort it; and if this *freedom* is rendered *equal* amongst all, by reducing *every one equally* under the control of law, thereby incapacitating each from impairing that freedom in another; then, the most important, the most extensive, the most attractive, the best defined portion of liberty is attained; the remainder can bear no comparison with it; it is of less extent, of less effect, of less consequence to the agency of man, or to the real and permanent interest of his being. He may doubtless pursue it, provided he does so with serious attention to the purpose of his creation, with faithful observance of the dictates of reason and conscience; and that he ever scrupulously compare the yearnings of

his

his desire, with the distinct unequivocal rule of duty, impressed upon his mind.

Having thus ascertained the nature of the right to *life*, and *liberty*; and having seen that they signify, " a right *common* to the human nature, " and therefore *equal* in every individual, to pre- " serve *life*, and to use it *freely*; except where " duty prescribes bounds to that use;" which seems to include every possible benefit that man can seek under the authority of natural right; we find no corner left for the distinct *right to equality*; the meaning of which words is indeed extremely perplexed, offering nothing precise, or that entitles it to a separate place in the class of natural rights. In the natures of men, all is inequality; to prevent the inconveniences and miseries resulting from thence, and to obtain equal security of life and of the use of life, was the end of civil government. What then is this *equality*, which is claimed on the ground of a natural right, inherent in every man? Do they who assert it, wish to abstract the relative notion of *equality* from *equal* security of life and liberty, and then to concoct it into an independent and positive entity? This would in truth be a desperate attempt of metaphysical sublimation. Do they mean to insinuate, that mankind, if set free from the control of government, would relapse into

an

an equality of powers and characters? But truth discovers to us, with every power of testimony, that without the control of government, the world must be a scene of the most disastrous inequality. Do they mean that every man is equally bound to discharge the obligation imposed upon man? that equal responsibility, equal necessity of answering to that responsibility, is annexed to each without exemption or distinction? This is most undeniably true; but if they mean this, it is the allegation of a *duty*, and not of a *right*. Do they mean that there is a *natural right* inherent in man, which is intrinsically and eternally repugnant to *civil distinctions* in states? If they mean this (and it is tolerably clear that this is what they wish to inculcate) it is a tangle of fallacy and inconsequence, occasioned by inaccuracy of thought and equivocation of terms, that calls for some temperate unravelling. Natural right is secured by the general performance of natural duty. The particular regulations of a government that provides effectually for the performance of every natural duty, in every part of the community, cannot invade any natural right. In the above perplexed proposition, in which *civil distinctions* are affirmed to be repugnant to *natural right*, two objects are confused, whose natures are intrinsically distinct. The notion of civil equality, implicated thus in the question of natural right, is in truth no question of natural right,* but of political convenience; and determinable by very different principles than those, by which the inquiry into

* We have already observed, and we may venture to repeat the observation, that the *natural right to equality*, or in terms more precise and intelligible, the *natural right to democracy* of the modern Jacobins, and the *divine right to absolute monarchy* of the old Jacobites, are notions that differ only in outward application, and not at all in intrinsic quality. If we compare, and attempt to generalise the two propositions, of a natural, indefeasible right to democracy, and a divine, indefeasible right to monarchy, we shall find, that they both flow into one common principle; namely, that there exists in the eternal and sovereign reason of the universe, an exclusive pattern or form for human society; precluding all liberty among mankind to deviate from that form; even though there should exist reasons of evident convenience, aptness, or even moral necessity for doing so. The maintainers of this doctrine, however, have been so unfortunate as to differ very widely (indeed as widely as opposite extremes can be) in their application of this arbitrary maxim; some applying it to the confluence of all the artificial powers of government into one individual person; others applying it to the diffusion of those same powers to every individual in the society; the one deriving effectual support to the ambition of a few aspiring individuals, from the irresistible energy of despotism; the other deriving an equally strong support to a few aspiring individuals, from the irresistible impetus of a multitude. Each reasoned with an equally grave plausibility from their common principle; the first alleging, that it is necessary for mankind to exist under a sufficient control, which can only be effected under an absolute monarchy; the second,

into the natural right of man is to be conducted. It is a question whether or not, in any given government, in which civil distinctions are admitted, the original end of government is truly attained. To decide which, we are to revert to the original design of government; for the government that best attains that end, will thereby approve itself to be the best constituted government, whatever artificial regulations it may have eventually admitted.

The object of government therefore, being (as has been shown) to obtain the discharge of duty

---

second, that man ought to exist under no more control than is sufficient, which can only be secured under a democracy. The first part of their positions is perfectly true, but they concluded very erroneously. Both were so far true, that it is right for man to exist under a sufficient control, and under no more control than is sufficient. But it happens, that democracy is by its nature hostile to the first of these, and absolute monarchy to the second. So that though each produced a reason invalidating the claim of the other, neither produced a reason establishing its own claim. All that followed was, therefore, that to obtain control sufficient, democracy ought to be avoided; and that to prevent that control from being more than sufficient, absolute monarchy ought to be avoided. And in this we discover, if not what particular compound of government is most conducive to the security and happiness of mankind, at least that it is neither absolute monarchy nor democracy; and consequently, that both Jacobite and Jacobin are equally unsupported by the ground, on which each have successively attempted to erect, their very different and discordant systems.

among mankind, in order to be able to acquire the happiness that can only be obtained by that process; if in any given country, whose internal polity has contrived artificial ranks and classes of subordination, it be questioned, whether such a contrivance invades the natural right of man; we are not to put the issue upon a general assent to, or dissent from the terms of the question, (which is the very matter in debate) but we are to examine and determine whether in that given country, the government established defends and secures the natural right of man; which if it does, the particular regulations of a country, in which the natural right of man is so secured, cannot, consistently with common sense, at the same time endanger them. For, if the means employed are such as evidently produce the end of government, and therefore secure man's natural right, it is quite impossible they should be at the same time *destructive* of the right they *secure*.

We cannot too often enforce, that the object of government is, to produce the discharge of those duties in each, which shall ensure to all the enjoyment of what they denominate their natural right. These duties, forming a part of that absolute and indefeasible obligation with which man is born, each one brings them with him into society; nor can any artificial or incidental circumstance of social life

life whatever, exonerate *any one* from that condition, to obtain the performance of which in *all,* is the very essence of association, the immutable purpose of all government. Because if *any* are exempted from the necessity of the obligation, in that proportion the success of the scheme of government is rendered abortive.

Every contrivance of government, every artificial regulation that societies may introduce, is to be estimated by its tendency to produce this general result. To devise an arrangement that might produce that result, was left to the labour and industry of man in every separate society. Different were the modes that each adopted, and accordingly as they were more or less apt to gain the purposed end, they succeeded or failed, they were continued or changed. The progress of experience improved the progress of civil polity; experimental good or evil guided each society in correcting or varying that which had proved inefficient to, or destructive of, the great interest of the union; and in proportion as any system improved, the discharge of duty in *every member* of the society, became more extended and more effectually ensured.

In the great comprehensive scheme of God, the discharge of duty is the *end* for which man was created;

created; it is the right of God's sovereignty, which overrules and determines every other consideration. The happiness to which, by God's goodness, that discharge leads, is anticipated by the heart of man, and is a powerful *means* contrived by the all-wise Creator, to allure him to that discharge. But in the partial scheme of civil government, the operation appears to be reversed. The happiness to which the nature of man tends; that happiness which is provided to be the result of the performance of duty, and to which he is intitled by the dispensation of the divine bounty; is the *end* designed by the institution; and the *means* employed to attain that end, are means calculated to produce the discharge of duty, as instrumental to that happiness. Here again we discover the necessary subordination of man's happiness, to which he alleges a right, to God's purpose, in which he is conscious of an obligation.

The perfect and entire discharge of duty, cannot be produced by the operation of any secondary and external causes. Near approximations are all that either wisdom expects, or nature allows. He who would be at the labour of searching for absolute perfection in human affairs, would resemble the simple boy who chased the rainbow; a meteor, the laws of whose being have nothing in common with

with the laws of substantial existence. Perfection in government, must ever be relative to the ability of procuring the most attainable degree of happiness among mankind, by means of the most practicable necessity to the discharge of duty.

The claim to perfection in any human government, must therefore produce evidence of these two things: first, that it is so constituted, as to include every attainable means for enforcing *universal obedience* of the duties that man owes to man, as instrumental to the general happiness; and to contain no principle tending to counteract its own end: secondly, that it be so constructed, and calculated in its different parts, as to promise *permanency*; since the *permanency* of happiness, is of absolute necessity to its *completion*.

The history of mankind is a history of governments, attended with more or less success, contrived with more or less effect to answer the end intended, and lasting a longer or a shorter time. In that instructive history, we are enabled to survey at leisure the different forms that government assumed in different societies, to trace the respective operations of each, the cause of its success, the occasion of its failure. In some, the power for compelling obedience was *insufficient*; in others, its operation

was

was *partial*; whereas in every one it ought to be, both *universal* and *complete*.

The machine of government, in its genuine design, supposes a force and a resistance. The *force* consists of an union of the natural powers of man under the guidance of reason, employed to overcome the *resistance* produced by similar powers under the instigation of passion. But the constituent parts of this machine, when considered in respect to practice, contain a radical imperfection which no human contrivance can ever remove; because it extends beyond the reach of human agency, and subsists in the very nature itself of man; in that defect of his nature, which alone rendered government necessary. If the force of government were to be exercised by Infinite Wisdom, as is implied in the true meaning of a theocracy, that imperfection, which more or less attends every possible form of human government, would not exist; because in that case government, which is designed to be exerted according to the rule of wisdom, would in reality be so exerted. But as soon as the scheme was attempted to be reduced to practice among men, the inherent defects of the individuals who were made the agents to conduct it, influenced the constituent parts of the machine, and produced a confusion and perplexity in the powers; by which

which event the unity of the original scheme was essentially impaired. For the force of government, which, in its genuine design, is a force intended to be exercised by the rule of wisdom, being consigned to an agent in which wisdom did not prevail, but who possessed that defective nature which called for the artificial control of government; the force that should have been directed by the rule of wisdom, was confided to the arm of passion, and was consequently abused from its original purpose, to the prejudice of those who confided it. And this occasioned a relative difference in the situation of the parties; for the breach of duty occurring in that part where the power for enforcing duty was confided, it remained for those who sought the real benefit of government to repair the breach thus made; which they could only do by encouraging the force of resistance in a proportionate degree, so as to counteract and repair the ill effects of this abuse of the force of government. And thus, a material change was introduced into the original scheme, two forces being produced acting with a continual reciprocating motion, one against the other. And, whatever inconvenience might attend the struggle, the nature of man rendered this reciprocation absolutely necessary, as being a less evil than that which it was designed to prevent. Wherefore, as every human government must be exercised by beings of the same common and imperfect nature, and which requires regulation and control in each, it is next to impossible to dispose force in such a manner, as to produce a reaction on those invested with it, and to keep them also under the constraint of positive obligation, without at the same time relaxing the due control of government over the mass of society. And yet, if this is not effected, the evil that results is, that either the force of government becomes insufficient, or its operation partial.

It is insufficient, whenever the resistance to be overcome is greater than the power that is to overcome it: Its operation is partial, whenever any are exempted from its effect.

The resistance to be overcome, is greater than the power that is to overcome it; whenever the means of enforcing duty are inferior to the means of transgressing it; that is, whenever the natural opposition to duty that government was instituted to overcome, is able to maintain itself against the efforts of government.

The natural opposition to duty is great or little, in proportion as the passions of those constituting the community are reduced under control; and that control

control is efficient, in proportion as it is able to maintain itself by means, independent of the paffions it is intended to reftrain. If the paffions of man had no other control, or but little other control, than the injunctions of duty and reafon; and if as foon as the authority of thefe fhould be contefted, the power of government would ceafe; there, the fcheme of government would be but a very trifling removal of man's condition from the fuppofed ftate of nature. Becaufe in the latter cafe, man would exift without any external conftraint over his paffions; and in the former, he would exift in a ftate in which he could prefently overcome any conftraint attempted to be exercifed over him.

Again, the operation of the force of government will be partial, where any are exempted from its effect.

This is the cafe whenever that force is exclufively difpofed in the hands of one, or of a certain limited number of individuals, fo that they who hold it, are thereby enabled to compel obedience in the general, while they themfelves are free from any fuch compulfion. When this cafe happens, the force created for the purpofe of producing general obedience, having no operation on the individuals who exercise it, and who are thereby emancipated from all constraint, becomes liable to be prostituted to the service of passion and personal interest in wrong of the public welfare; and the excess of strength it superadds to the natural powers of man, partially revives the inequality of nature, and aids them more effectually to trespass upon the interests of others, who are by this means abridged of even the natural powers of resistance.

So that, when the fear of confiding to the artificial organ, a force sufficient to restrain the action of passion, leaves the controlling power of government inefficient, passion is ever liable to prevail; the natural disorder of mankind that government aims at repressing, is at all times liable to break forth; and of course, law and order to be dissolved, and anarchy to ensue. On the other hand, when force is so absolutely and exclusively abandoned to the artificial organ, that there remains no power to restrain the operation of passion acting in the human subjects composing that organ; there, passion, which is the proper object of government, is enabled to act without restraint; and being invigorated by an adventitious strength produces despotism or tyranny. Such have been the case more or less whenever the scheme of government

ment has contained within itself a principle, destructive of its genuine purpose. The former, existing in its fullest defect is, the case of absolute democracy; the latter, existing in their fullest defects are, cases of absolute monarchy, and absolute aristocracy.

In the first case, the body of resistance is too great for the power that is opposed to it; in the latter, the operation of that power, which ought to be equally directed upon all, is diverted from influencing upon some, and its weight falls with increased, undiscriminating violence, upon the remainder.

To correct those evils, wise men laboured from the beginning of society; while from the same æra, wicked men struggled hard to perpetuate them.

They who endeavoured to correct the evils of absolute democracy, imagined various counteracting powers to repress the turbulence of the mass. They who endeavoured to correct the evils of the two other forms, sought, on the contrary, the means of giving energy and effect to the natural vigour of the mass. They pursued and tried every possible relation and proportion between force and resist-

resistance; but in the two compound quantities which they thus endeavoured to regulate, and into which the political machine was divided, a constant fluctuation and variation took place. They laboured to adjust the balance; but if ever it was nearly effected, a grain added to either side occasioned a preponderance. They were wanting in some certain means for preserving the equilibrium in the state; and thus the restlessness of man, acting vigorously in two opposite relations, kept up an unceasing transfer of weight from the one side to the other; and the affairs of human society partook of the evils attending either the reciprocation of the balance, or the preponderance of either scale.

To put an end to these disorders, by obtaining some principle of government that should be at all times able to repel them, became an object of anxious desire to the most enlightened minds; who, knowing equally well how to estimate the value of legal restraint as of rational liberty, and possessing full experience of the forms and effects of every different government that the world had witnessed, yearned for some one, which, while it possessed the advantages of each, should be at the same time radically exempt from all their defects.

Neither Greece nor Rome, the great champions of liberty and oracles of civil polity, were able to accomplish that medium. Their states rose and sunk, sometimes by the weight of democracy, sometimes by that of aristocracy, sometimes by that of autocracy. The reflective experience of which calamitous proofs of the incapacity, of any of those forms of polity, however modified or contorted, to procure the full measure of the benefits of civil government, and to secure their stability, drew from the pens of two of the wisest men that ever reflected honour upon their species, those short but pregnant and memorable sentiments, never to be too often or too deeply imprinted on the memories of Englishmen.

" That (said Cicero) would, in my opinion, be
" the best possibly constituted state, which should
" consist of a moderate commixture of the three
" kinds of governments, regal, noble, and
" popular."

And at the distance of a century and a half from Cicero, Tacitus, though he despaired of its practicability, and therefore banished all expectation of seeing it realised, still maintained the same opinion. " All nations (says he) have been hitherto go-
" verned, either by the mass, or by a few leaders,

" or

" or by individual governors. A form of government constituted by selection from each of these, would rather be a subject of mental admiration than of probable occurrence; or if it did take place, it could not be of long continuance."

So thought those two great reasoners on government. They had never seen such a government; they had no prospect of seeing such a government; but their perfect knowledge of past events, and of the nature and practice of human society; the instructions of their wisdom, and their unqualified attachment to truth; obliged them to infer, that the evils attending every other form of government that man had devised, could only be radically cured or prevented, by establishing government on an union of the principles of these three several forms; the seeds of each of which exist in every state, because in every state the interests of liberty, property, and security subsist; all of which are best attained, and best advanced, by such a form of polity: disposing them in such a manner, as to procure every benefit peculiarly resulting from each, and at the same time to repress the evils to which each might particularly give rise: and so distributing the supreme power between them, that each should counterpoise another, and a third at all times maintain the equipoise between two, whenever

ever it should be in danger of being disturbed. By these means, control, the great object of government would be easily and naturally produced in each constituent part of the state; each would be contained within the limits assigned by the law, without straining the political machine, or burthening it with any complex and excrescent machineries, tending always to impede or perplex its necessary motions. For, as the failure in the original scheme of government was owing to the irregular struggle between two contending quantities, moved by contrary interests and jealousies, and acting in direct and constant opposition the one to the other; and as such struggle either became perpetual, thus perpetuating internal broil and confusion; or was terminated by the preponderance of one or other power, thus fixing different proportions of anarchy or tyranny; there was no method left for remedying those evils, than in altogether removing the cause producing them; by making a new distribution of the powers and interests that civil government introduces among men; and disposing them in such a manner that the evils of the old distribution should never be able to return, and that a portion of force should always subsist, capable of giving effectual succour to that side, which, in the event of opposition between two powers, should endeavour to maintain the great objects of duty and right,

right, the ultimate purpose for which government was originally contrived. And, in order to prevent partial interest in the exercise of these several alotments of power, from operating to the prejudice of of the public good, but, on the contrary, to render the activity of private interest, which can never be extinguished in man, instrumental to the public welfare, and an active principle to advance the motion of the state; it followed, that it would be altogether necessary to annex particular interests to each, in such a manner, as that an attempt in any one to disturb the arrangement established, would impair the respective interests of the other two, and thereby impel them to unite in resistance of the violence attempted; thus producing a force at all times superior to the most vigorous opposition, that any one could make against them: and further, that the particular interests thus respectively attached to each, should be such as together to constitute the general interests of all; for the vigilance with which each would maintain the appropriate interest in which it was more especially concerned, would not only keep each from following the declination of either of the other powers, and cause it to adhere strenuously to the sphere assigned it; but the great aggregate interest, in respect to which society is established, and according to the cultivation of which, society becomes powerful and refined, would be defended and promoted with all the zeal, that the energy of private interest, or of individual gratification, can possibly contribute. By dividing, therefore, the supreme power of government into three equal portions of force, an equipoise could be ensured in its machinery; and by annexing specially to each of these, one of the three leading interests of society, that machinery would invariable act in furtherance of the public interest.

The leading interests in society appear to be reducible to three general heads; liberty, property, and security. Liberty, is an interest equal in every individual, and annexed to our common nature by its Author. It consists in the free use of life, and of the faculties of life, except where the will of the Author has prescribed bounds to that use. Property, is an interest arising out of the exertion and industry of man in society, and is the object of all human action; it consists " in the enjoy-
" ment and disposal of *our acquisitions*, without
" any control or diminution, save only by the law
" of the land." Security, is the great interest pursued in the establishment of civil government, and without which, liberty and property can scarcely be said to exist at all. It consists in the actual application of power to repress all causes

tending to endanger either liberty or property, and which therefore establishes in the minds of all, that repose and confidence which is absolutely necessary to the complete enjoyment of either.

If, now, a due adaptation were made of these three leading interests of society, to each of the three constituent parts of the government here supposed with peculiar motives urging each to the particular preservation of its respective interest; the action of the three powers, in relation to the general interest, would be ensured, by the vigour with which each would maintain its separate interest; and which, at the same time, by means of the counteraction of the other two, it would never be able to extend to a degree injurious to the rest.

As this cannot be placed in too strong light of evidence, let us consider again the scheme of government here suggested to our imagination. What we are to observe in it is, the *number* and *quality* of the organs, among which the sovereign power is proposed to be distributed. And that which presents itself first to our contemplation is the *number*, or the distribution of the energies of the state into *three* portions; instead of into *two*, as it must necessarily be in every other system, excepting such as as are absolutely despotic. The immediate consequence of this division of supreme legislative power into three equal parts is, that no one constituent part possesses more than one third of that power, consequently, that no one can exert more power than in that proportion. The first effect of this reduction of the *quantity* of power in the organs of the state, by increasing their *number*, is, to produce immediately that quiet and repose, which was in vain sought for while the whole power was contested by two active and hostile interests, both inclined, and able, to maintain a perpetual contention. For the comparative weakness of each of the three powers, rendering it unable to cope with two other powers, each equal to itself, would dispose each to remain quiet within its sphere; or, if either should make any attempt to exceed it, the double force of the resisting powers would presently reduce it within its equal bounds. Hence a principle of *repose*, or internal quiet, is obtained by this simple operation, which no other division of that power could possibly effect. But as these three constituent divisions of the sovereign power are to *act* * for the welfare of the whole; and as

* " Ces trois puissances devroient former un *repos* ou une
" *inaction*. Mais comme, par le movement nécessaire des
" choses, elles feront contraintes *d'aller*, elles feront forcées
" *d'aller en concert.*" Esprit des Loix. l. xi. c. 6.

the union of their several acts is to constitute the act of the whole, or the law; it is necessary that all should be actuated by an identity of interest, in order that all may conspire to the general end. And yet, as it is of principal necessity to the maintenance of the threefold division of power, that the several organs invested with that power should continue ever intrinsically distinct (otherwise there would be an end to the threefold division intended) and that they should be incapable of ever coalescing, or uniting into one; it is necessary that all should be actuated by a diversity of interests, tending to keep them ever distinct and apart the one from the other. Thus each, as by a species of centrifugal force, yielding to a particular impulse; and again, by a species of centripetal attraction, compelled to adhere to the general interests of the community. And in such a government as is here suggested, these necessities singularly concur. For, as in all states, as we have observed, the interests of liberty, property, and security subsist, and constitute the interests of all; so, in this particular state, besides the interest which all possess in common in these particulars, each of the three supposed organs possesses a distinct and powerful incentive for pursuing one of these in particular. This will be perceived if we consider the *quality* of the organs

sup-

supposed in this hypothesis; which are, popular, noble, and regal.

As in such a government, in which power would subsist in an equal degree in each division of the state, each would equally concur to create the law; so the law would be sure to influence equally upon each, and no exemption would be allowed to any. In such a system, therefore, there would be but one general rule or law for liberty, one general rule for property, and one general rule for security; and the mode that best defended each, would best protect all. *Liberty* is immediately endangered, when power grows excessive in any supreme constituent function; *property* is immediately endangered, either when artificial power grows excessive in any particular function; or, when the boundaries of law are threatened, and the defences set to property invaded, by the eruption of the natural passions of mankind; *security* is endangered, when those whom the law is designed to repress, acquire a preponderating force over the energy of the law. The jealousy with which the popular part, or the bulk of society, acting by that organ of representation which every democratic body must possess, would resist every encroachment on liberty, would establish the best protection that the natural interest of liberty can possess, against any effort or exertion made on the part of power.

The jealousy with which the opulent nobles (who constitute the second organ here supposed) would naturally defend, with the power vested in them, their large share of that general capital which is the object of common concern, and in the perpetual circulation of which consists the prosperity of the whole community; would be the most secure protection that the artificial interest of *property* could possess, against either excess of power tending to regal confiscation; or the eruption of popular passion, producing democratic plunder. The jealousy and vigilance with which the regal organ would defend its individual capacity, the source of all political action, against any illegal force usurping upon its authority, would be the best pledge of *security*; which is only to be obtained by an alert and strenuous exertion of the calculated powers vested in it by the law.

In a government thus compounded, we are not only to compute the quantity of good that each of the three general qualities can contribute; we are also to ascertain the particular evils that each might occasion, and to provide effectually against them. In the regal estate, we have to guard against the excess of power, which constitutes the evil of absolute monarchy; in the popular part, we are to guard against that turbulence of passion, which is

the

the inherent malady of all democracy. A due reduction of the power of the former, establishes liberty, and with it security, in all: a due constraint of the violence of the latter, produces security, and with it liberty, for all. If however, the force of either of the two exceed its bounds, and become exercised in respect to individual interest; whether it be the interest of the few supported by monarchical power, or the interest of the many supported by democratical vehemence, the great interest of property, which is the basis of all regular, industrious, prosperous and polished society, is endangered. This great interest of property, therefore, becomes invariably and exclusively united with power, in the intermediate order, and is thus equally defended against kingly plunder, and democratical equalization. So that we may venture to affirm, that of these three several functions, that whose means of benefiting, infinitely overweighs its ability of injuring society, is that of the nobles; because, at the same time that it contributes as much as either of its coequals, to maintain the equilibrium of power, and to secure the equality of law, it contains no feed of strength, tending either to cramp liberty by the abuse of law, or to subvert law by the explosion of human passions. It thus stands a mediator, establishing peace and amity between the energies of regal and popular power.

power. It is, in a manner, the key-stone, that binds the triumphal arch, springing from the opposite bases of monarchy and democracy.

The good effect of this machinery once set in action, was manifest to the minds of those great men. The partition of powers; the opposition of particular interests, producing necessarily the establishment of the general interest; would unavoidably secure at all times a majority of strength on the side of duty, and proportionably diminish the power of resistance on the side of passion. The same motive for disturbing the machine, could never actuate two of the powers at the same time, because their particular interests would be distinct; and yet the common interest of preserving the machine would always actuate the two that found an enemy in the third. Whereever resistance to the scheme of government discovered itself in the proportion of one third, coercive power would be able to exert itself in the proportion of two thirds. If the resistance showed itself in the regal part, the middle and popular part would reduce it; if it appeared in the popular part, the regal and middle would constrain it; if in the middle, the regal and popular would overcome it. And thus, each being compellible by the fundamental principle of the polity to discharge the duties of the artificial

sphere

sphere contrived for each, none would be exempted from the operation of that necessity, and the result would be universal obedience, as far as the nature of man will allow; and its produce would be those enjoyments of existence, which naturally flow from thence, and which compose what are called in popular phrase, the natural rights of man. And under the enjoyment of these, the united industry and talents of each would be enabled to multiply and cultivate those other subordinate enjoyments, which he calls his civil rights. And it is a very reasonable presumption, that the government that best attains the general end of its institution, will provide also the best store of social benefits, or civil rights: for it can only attain the general end, by a strict observance of wisdom and justice; and wisdom and justice are all that is required, to establish civil rights on the best and most prosperous foundation.

To the conscience of every Englishman we now appeal; to that honour, that frankness and honesty, which, we fain would flatter ourselves, stamps the character of Englishmen; to them we ask—*Where* has such a government been found?—*What social fruits* has that government produced?

Did it exist in Egypt or the East; in Greece or in Rome? No! it was at best a phantom in the minds of their wifeſt philoſophers; a point of imaginary perfection, to which they hardly could allow themſelves to hope, that human nature would, in practice, ever be able to attain.

Did it ſucceed to the ſubverſion of empire in Rome, and eſtabliſh itſelf on the ruins of imperial tyranny? Alas! the various ſhapes of deſpotiſm or licentiouſneſs, that ſprung from the ruin of the empire, ſhowed how ill it was to be procured by turbulence or war. Did it any where attempt to gain as real and ſubſtantial exiſtence? If ſuch efforts it ſeemed here and there to make, they proved abortive; the balance was preſently turned, and the ſcale fixed by the preponderance of one or other of the powers.

There remained however one great and illuſtrious exception, one brilliant and ſingle inſtance of ſucceſs amidſt the general failure. This principle of government, the faireſt offspring of wiſdom and of juſtice, involved itſelf in the origin of civilization in England, and accompanied its progreſs through every modification of its polity. It influenced every act tending to the public good; and if at any time the equilibrium was loſt by the vacillation of the balance, this principle reſtored it; it brought the ſcales by degrees to an exact and

perfect

perfect equipoise; and at length fixed the beam, so that no moderate convulsion could turn it.

From the commencement of our history, we discover the principle of the partition of powers; of the opposition of partial interests, producing the security of the aggregate interest; of that tripartite distribution of power, which only can effectually and certainly ensure to duty and right, a force at all times equal to their defence. In the progress of that history, we have proof of the salutary effect of this arrangement, in the boundaries at different times assigned to those different powers; by sometimes abscinding from the one and adding to the other, according as experimental necessity directed; until at length their due relative proportions were accurately defined and fixed, by the truly glorious and happy revolution of 1688. An event, how much more justly to be remembered with pious gratitude, and commemorated with patriotic ardor, by Englishmen, than any *one* of the *three* revolutions of France, during the last *seven years*, by the ill-fated victims of their fury!

Such is the nature of the government subsisting in England. It provides a universal control over all who are subject to it, whether king, peerage, or commons: for king, peers, and commons, are

equally

equally subject to that rule, which is paramount over all. As far as human nature can allow it, as far as any effect can be perfect, of which man is the instrument or medium, the constitution of this government is perfect. Some of those defects which will ever adhere to works of human execution, may doubtless be discoverable even here; but it contains within itself a correcting energy, acting always up to the measure of experimental necessity. That principle which was coeval with its origin, and attendant on every step of its progress, still animates its system; it is immortal and exhaustless as the immutable wisdom from whence it springs; and if we desert not it, it never will desert us.

It presents to all, a full measure of the fruits of accomplished government, namely, *equal necessity to duty—equal security of right*. The inevitable consequence of that moderating system of legislation is, a corresponding moderation and equality in the administration of the laws provided. Each interest contributing equally to make the law, no artificial function is exempted from that necessity to duty, no individual person is excluded from that equal security of right. Neither wealth nor privilege, poverty nor obscurity, furnishes the least exception from the former; on the other hand, equal security
of

of right is extended to all. He who toils in the meanest office of society, stands on the same level with the prince of the sovereign's blood, in the sacred eye of the law. Though the scheme of government requires, for the existence and motion of its machineries, the contrivance of different degrees of subordination, yet the result of the whole is, security and protection dealt out equally to each. The honest avowal of a distinguished foreign writer, the native of a republic, is perhaps one of the most satisfactory evidences that can be produced to Englishmen, of the inestimable blessings they possess in the administration of the laws of their country. " The singular situations of the
" English judges relatively to the three constituent
" powers of the state,—has at last created such
" an impartiality in the distribution of public
" justice in England,—and procured to every in-
" dividual, both such an easy access to the courts
" of law, and such a certainty of redress, as are
" not to be paralleled in any other government.
" Philip de Comines, so long as three hundred
" years ago, commended in strong terms the
" exactness with which justice is done in England
" to all ranks of subjects; and the impartiality
" with which the same is administered in these
" days, will with still more reason create the sur-
" prise of every stranger, who has an opportunity of
" ob-

"observing the customs of this country.*" Such is the blessing exceeding all calculation, which we derive from the administration of public justice, "relatively (as this writer well remarks) to the three "constituent powers of the state." If we were to allow any one of these constituent powers to be in the least impaired, a change in that admirable system of justice, entailing consequences affecting us all, must be the certain result.

But, besides that the English constitution produces effectually the *universality of obedience*, and thereby the *stability* of society, it also provides for its own *permanency*. It is a self-preservative, self-acting principle; another circumstance that we have stated to be necessary to the perfection of government, and to the completion of that happiness which government endeavours to establish. For the same commanding reason, that directs to the proper means for obtaining the end of government; and that has rendered the permanency of happiness essential to its completion; requires, that the means for obtaining the great end of social security, when once successfully contrived, shall also be rendered *permanent*.

*De Lolme, *On the Const. of England.* p. 376. See the note he subjoins to the passage here quoted.

The permanency of civil government, is beſt ſought for in the perpetuation of that which produced its ſtability. This, as we have ſeen, was the threefold diſtribution of power, by the inſertion of a moderating quantity, capable at all times of producing an equipoiſe. The Engliſh polity, produces the ſtability of government by its actual operation; it ſecures its permanency by its fundamental conſtitution.

That this ſtability ſhould become permanent, it is neceſſary that the means producing the ſtability ſhould be continued without interruption. Theſe means conſiſt of the mutual action and concurrence of the three ſeveral branches, among which the ſupreme power has been equally divided. The permanency of the popular part, is effected by the common operation of the laws of nature, by which a conſtant ſucceſſion in the human race is maintained, and it is thus that the popular intereſt is rendered perpetual. As the powers of the two other parts are to be exerciſed by men, and the life of man is precarious and ſhort; and as it is eſſential to the threefold diſtribution of power, that each be equal to the other in every reſpect, not only in actual, but alſo in continuing, uninterrupted energy; the example of nature is followed, and perpetuity is communicated to the two other branches

branches of the state, on the same principle of hereditary succession. Not devised, as pride and envy endeavour to persuade, with the sole view of creating invidious and partial benefits; but for the wise and salutary purpose of continuing, without interruption, the operation of a cause, that produces and confirms every possible advantage of civil government. By means of hereditary succession of their respective qualities and characters, in all the three constituent parts of the government, a constant and equal process of every part of the political machinery is secured. Every inconvenience flowing to the practical use of civil government from the brevity of human life, by which the wisest contrivances are defeated, and the periodical return of civil disorder produced, is by this means totally prevented. Distant ages, that the term of human life is unable to connect, are by this contrivance connected; and posterity is thus ensured of the transmission of those benefits, with unalterable identity, which wisdom and virtue have bled to procure. A perpetual interest is maintained, supplying the energies of civil government with perpetual vigour. And thus the three constituent portions of the state, each united in itself, and all compacted with each other; possessing the same inherent strength of nature, and endowed with the same principle of perpetuity; establish that strong, com-

plex

plex, indissoluble chain, which holds the constitution, during the tide of centuries, firm to the soil of England, securing its identity, while it establishes its permanency.*

Such are the benefits we derive from this triple arrangement of power; the evidence of which has forcibly affected all those philosophers who have directed their attention to observe it. "This," says the celebrated Montesquieu, "is the funda-
"mental constitution of the government of which
"we are speaking. The legislative body being
"composed of two parts, the one will control the
"other by its power of negativing; and both
"these will be controled by the executive branch,
"which in its turn will also control the two legis-
"lative branches. The three powers would
"therefore produce a repose, or inaction; but
"since, by the unavoidable course of things, they
"will be obliged to act, they will thus be under
"the necessity of acting in concert."† "If this
"power had only been divided into two parts,"
(says De Lolme) "it is probable they would not
"in all cases unite, either for doing or undoing:—

* So that we may apply to it Chrysippus's definition of fate: "Sempiterna quædam et indeclinabilis series rerum et catena," &c. Aul: Gell: L. vi. c. 2.
† Spirit of Laws. B. xi. c. 6,

"if it has been divided into three parts, the chance that no change will be made is thereby greatly increased."* And here we may by the way observe, that by being divided into *three parts*, must be meant, in common reason, *three equal parts*. For, unless the power be distributed in every respect *equally* to *each* of the *three*, so that each be absolutely and equally independent one of the other in the exercise of that power, and also equally permanent, nothing is done; nor can the arithmetic of *three* transmit any virtue to the *triple distribution* of power, unless upon this principle of *equal distribution*: for, in which ever of these points one of the three is radically inferior to the others, whether it be in the quantity of power, in its absolute occupation, or in its permanency, in that point an excess is given to one or both of the others; the equilibrium, which alone was sought for in this tripartite division, is *ipso facto* destroyed; and it matters very little then, how many nominal or ostensible shapes the pageant of government assumes. Such is the case of France, who, in order to comply in outward exhibition with the peremptory voice of reason and experience, has now split her democracy into three ostensible portions. But as these do not all stand on the same foundation, of equality

* De Lolme. B. ii. c. 3.

of legislative power, of independency and permanency, it is not faithfully divided according to the rule pretended. But, with respect to us, "The "legislature of the kingdom is intrusted to three "distinct powers, entirely independent of each "other; first, the King; secondly, the Lords— "and, thirdly the House of Commons. As this "aggregate body, actuated by different springs, "and attentive to different interests, composes the "British Parliament, and has the supreme dis- "posal of every thing; there can no inconvenience "be attempted by either of the three branches, "but will be withstood by one of the other two; "each branch being armed with a negative power, "sufficient to repel any innovation which it shall "think inexpedient or dangerous."

"Here then is lodged the sovereignty of the "British constitution; and lodged as beneficially "as possible for society. For in no other shape "could we be so certain of finding the three great "qualities of government so well and so happily "united. If the supreme power was lodged in "any one of the three branches separately, we "must be exposed to the inconveniences of either "absolute monarchy, aristocracy, or democracy; "and so want two of the three principal ingredients "of good polity, either virtue, wisdom, or power.

" If it were lodged in any one of the two branches;
" for inſtance in the king and houſe of lords, our
" laws might be providently made, and well exe-
" cuted, but they might not always have the
" good of the people in view: if lodged in the
" king and commons, we ſhould want that cir-
" cumſpection and mediatory caution, which the
" wiſdom of the peers is to afford: if the ſupreme
" rights of legiſlature were lodged in the two houſes
" only, and the king had no negative upon their
" proceedings, they might be tempted to incroach
" upon the royal prerogative, or perhaps to aboliſh
" the kingly office, and thereby weaken (if not
" totally deſtroy) the ſtrength of the executive
" power. But the conſtitutional government of
" this iſland is ſo admirably tempered and com-
" pounded, that nothing can endanger or hurt it,
" but deſtroying the equilibrium of power between
" one branch of the legiſlature and the reſt. For
" if ever it ſhould happen that the independence
" of one of the three ſhould be loſt, or that it
" ſhould become ſubſervient to the views of either
" of the other two, there would ſoon be an end of
" the conſtitution.*"

And as each of theſe three is eſpecially moved to adhere to one of the three leading intereſts of ſociety, the popular part being the ſtrenuous defenders of

indi-

* Blackſtone's Comm. b. i.

individual *liberty* in particular; the nobles being the jealous protectors of opulence, and all its advantages, and therein at the same time of *property in general*, and all its enjoyments;* there being but one law for property in all its various degrees of

---

* It is worthy of remark here, that the first great security obtained for the property of every denomination of persons in the realm, and that, too, at a time when the bulk of the people were immersed in vassalage and slavery, was procured by the jealousy with which the rich barons surveyed the arbitrary character of the Crown. It was to them that the nation owed the *great Charter of Liberties*, by which the property of every Englishman was placed upon the same level of security; and (to use the words of the excellent Blackstone) it did that " which alone would have merited the title that it bears, of " the *great Charter*, it protected every individual of the nation " in the free enjoyment of his life, his liberty, and his pro- " perty, unless declared to be forfeited by the judgment of his " peers, or the law of the land." At a much later period of our history, when the abuse of the kingly power had given way to the abuse of the democratic power, of the constitution; the peerage of the realm opposed the career of the latter, as in the time of John they had opposed the conduct of the Crown. But the Crown being then extinguished, the peerage became only the weaker of two contending powers, and were soon abolished, and voted to be useless and dangerous, by those, who desired to sway without control. In which histories, we may remark, first, the benefit of the intermediate body of the nobles, while the state remained entire; and secondly, the facility with which the whole fabric of the constitution was overturned, as soon as an infraction was made into any of its parts.

the

wealth or competency; and the king being, by the unity of his political capacity, the vigilant and effectual maintainer of the force of government, by which *security* is produced; and in maintaining which, the dignity, and safety, no less of his person than of his office, entirely depends; it becomes morally impossible that any one should abandon its particular interests, and consequently that the interest of the whole should not be fully promoted.

The constitution of England, however, while it has established itself on the general plan first commended by Cicero, has infinitely refined upon the general principle, by the admirable constitutions of the regal, mediatory, and representative organs of legislation; (absolutely in themselves, and relatively to each other;) and by the delegation of all the executive power to a single individual, who is kept in check by the entire reserve of the treasure of the country to the disposal of the great councils of the nation, with different degrees of power: thus adapting its parts so exquisitely the one to the other, that they appear to blend into a perfect whole, in which the radical diversity of interests are with difficulty distinguished: each constituent part being rendered susceptible of the interests of each, and in a manner an epitome of the whole.

But

But this permanency of government, which wisdom calls for as indispensable to its perfection, is disclaimed by our antagonists as essentially contrary to their "rights of man". Those rights, say they, protest against any restriction being imposed by one generation upon another. Here we again discover, with amazement and with grief, the snare woven by knavery, to entrap inadvertency and simplicity. Had government no better foundation on which it could rest than the caprice of man, their objection would be admissible; because no man is obliged to submit to the caprice of another. But as every man is born the subject of Infinite Wisdom; as he is bound in his nature by an absolute and indefeasible obligation to the will of God; and is severely accountable for his observance of the rule prescribed by it; as civil government acts on behalf of that wisdom, and in conformity with that rule; and as the authority of wisdom is in every age unalterably the same; it signifies nothing in what specific generation the injunctions of wisdom received the sanction of human laws. In order, therefore, to be free from so embarrassing a rule, and to leave the door open to the continual action of interest and passion, these have endeavoured to persuade, that government has no rule but the *will* of the community, thereby intending to give force to the *absolute will of man*, independently of every moral rule. And to this hypothesis they have adapted all their reasoning. But if this principle were admitted, man's right would extend to prevent the continuance of any institution that wisdom might enjoin; and the speculations of every race, being backed by an alleged right to make experiment of those speculations, the best efforts of wisdom might be over-ruled by the operation of a principle, pretended to be implanted by wisdom herself; than which nothing can well be more preposterous and absurd. Such a right would, in effect, be a right to maintain an unceasing revolution of human affairs; and the right of one generation, following close upon that of the preceding one, the old age of man would have no ground for hoping, that it should enjoy the continuation of that which his manhood had laboured to establish; there having sprung up a new right with power, capable of over-ruling the bare right, which the decrepitude of age now left destitute of support. Thus, the duration of governments would merely extend from the age of vigour in one generation, to the age of vigour in another; and their stability would remain to be computed by the longevity of man in each, determinable only by their respective bills of mortality.

On such a foundation would rest the whole fabric of society, the whole apparatus of government, if there were not some secure ground, some solid *substratum*, immoveable by any plea of right in man; on which such plea must depend; and which, in the event of opposition, must quash every plea of right set up by man. Such a ground is wisdom; enjoining strict observance of the rule of duty, thence deducing the notion of right in man; and directing to an union of the natural energies of man, to compel observance of that rule, thence to acquire the natural objects of that right. This is the only true and genuine nature of government, which is more or less good, not as it agrees or disagrees with arbitrary and indistinct notions of right; but, as it is more or less capable of securing the end sought for by its institution.

Until a remote view of the coruscations proceeding from the conflagration of the ancient monarchy of France, was mistaken by many for the dawning lustre of a brighter day, we were all accustomed to believe, that this great object was attained, and in a manner almost miraculous, under our revered constitution. There are still many, very many, who hold this opinion unshaken; who have been proof against the short-lived illusion.

These conceive, that the pole star of wisdom, by which the helm of Britain has been steered during a boisterous voyage of many centuries, and by means of which the sacred vessel was at length prosperously brought to her moorings in the haven of the Revolution, presents to all mankind, but experimentally to Britons, a far securer guidance than the incendiary blaze of France, however its glare may sensibly exceed in intensity, or its apparent diameter in magnitude.

We shall enter into no further examination of the peculiar excellencies of the constitution, first, because it would extend this address beyond all consistent bounds; secondly, because we have done all that we were desirous of doing, by showing that the English constitution establishes that equal necessity to obey the force of government in every individual, which is the object of all government, and that it does this solely by the triple and equal distribution of its legislative power; but lastly, and most particularly, because that work is already greatly accomplished, and by talents widely different from ours. Were those invaluable productions as industriously consulted, as the scurrilous and lying ribaldry disseminated by the friends of disorder; the constitution would become an object of far more enthusiastic admiration, than

than it has ever yet been of obloquy and abuse. To those sound and persuasive writers, let us direct the attention of every description of Englishmen; those particularly, who feel an anxiety to form an opinion of the constitution, or a desire to pronounce a judgment upon it; but most especially those, who have joined in the uproar and clamor that ignorance, yielding itself to the authority of treason, has so zealously raised against it. There they will discover, with wonder and with indignation, that they have been made the dupes of the most hollow and unsubstantial artifice that was ever exercised over the understandings of mankind. There they will discover, that what has been held forth to them as an object deserving only of their contempt, their suspicion, and disgust; will transfix them by the evidence of its worth, and fulfil them with confidence, with affection, and respect: They will soon be convinced, that those who slandered their birthrights and the source of their security, had their secret reasons for being the enemies of their birthrights and security; and if they cannot exactly trace the specific interest that each pursued by such a proceeding, they will at least detect the spirit of treachery and villany that conspired their destruction. To those oracles, therefore, of fair and honest reasoning, those just and faithful expositors of the laws and constitution of his country, we

refer

refer every inquiring Briton;* satisfying ourselves with producing here only one authority, but which is qualified for this selection by the particular character of the man, whose writings have eminently tended to raise that perturbed and unhallowed spirit, which, from the heart of France, his native country, now diffuses melancholy and distress over the whole face of Christendom.

"We may believe," says this writer, "that a
"constitution which has regulated the rights of the
"king, of the nobles, and of the people, and in
"which each finds his security, will last as long as
"any thing human can last. We may further
"believe, that all states that are not founded on
"similar principles, must undergo revolutions."

"The government of England has attained
"this object by instating men in all those natural
"rights of which they are abridged in almost
"every monarchy. These rights are, entire liberty
"of his person and property; the liberty of ad-
"dressing the nation in writing; of not being
"judged in any criminal matter otherwise than
"by a jury composed of independent men; of

* See Blackstone's *Commentaries* Vol. I. De Lolme, on *The Constitution of England.* Paley's *Moral Philosophy*, Vol. II. b. 6. Montesquieu's *Spirit of Laws*, b. 11.

"being

" being, in no case, otherwise judged than accord-
" ing to the strict terms of the law; of peaceably
" professing any religion, with the sole condition
" of foregoing those particular situations which
" are set apart for the established church. These
" are styled *prerogatives*; and it is in truth a very
" great and happy prerogative, over and above
" most nations of the earth, for a man to be sure
" in going to bed that he shall rise in the morn-
" ing master of the same property he then pos-
" sessed; that he shall not be torn from the arms
" of his wife, from his children, in the middle of
" the night, to be conveyed to a dungeon or a de-
" sert; that in rising from his bed he shall have the
" power of publicly exposing his thoughts; that
" if he is accused of any crime, either by act, by
" speech, or by writing, that he shall only be
" judged according to law. And this prerogative
" extends its foot to every one who sets his foot
" in England. A foreigner enjoys equally the
" liberty of his person and property; and if he is
" accused, he may demand that half his jurors
" should be also foreigners.

" I will venture to affirm, that if the whole
" race of men were assembled for the purpose of
" making laws, they would be formed after this
" model for the general security."*

* Voltaire, *Dict. Philosoph. Gouvernment.*

Such is the condition, under which that portion of mankind who inhabit the British islands, enjoy by God's good providence their favoured existence! such is the result of that coincidence of circumstances, which has conspired to place their country on the pinnacle of the world; and which has rendered Great Britain the mediating power in the scale of nations, to which all look for the preservation of the rights and liberties established among states. To every Englishman, the constitution of his country is his dearest and most valuable possession; it is his *right* to hold and to preserve it. But it is also the right of his posterity, intrusted to his care; it is therefore his *duty* to honour and to defend it. It is an efficient engine in his own hand, the best that the united labours of reason and experience have yet been able to produce, for acquiring the most practicable happiness that the short life of man can ever hope to taste. It is his right to defend it, as he defends his castle; but what is of far prior importance, it is his bounden duty to defend it.

There is an expedient, congenial to their natures, to which the adversaries of the constitution have ready recourse, in order to repress any movements YOU might be disposed to make to control the activity of treason; and that is, by representing all

such

such efforts as engaged in the support of tyranny, and having for their ultimate object to extend the power of the Crown; thus repelling the charge of treason by the counter-charge of servility. And if such a stratagem could be successful; if conscious integrity were unable to maintain itself against conscious crime; if the courage of virtue could not cope with the courage of guilt, nothing more would be required to extinguish the constitution, and to accomplish the scheme of anarchy and desolation. As soon as Englishmen shall be deterred, by the lofty tone of traitors, from engaging openly and boldly in the cause of duty; as soon as the fear of enduring that imputation which their hearts repel, shall overcome their propensity to discharge that duty which their hearts enjoin; as soon as juries shall imbibe the fatal maxim, that the crime of treason is of so indefinite and doubtful a quality, as to deserve by every possible contrivance to be rescued from the rigour of the law; and as soon as it shall be radicated in the minds of the multitude, that though it is the duty of every one to bring forth to justice, him who steals to satisfy the cries of hunger in an impoverished family, it is yet infamous, and an offence against all society, to inform against him who endeavours to plunge society itself into misery and blood; as soon as all these things shall be accomplished, the triumph of treason will be completed, and the period of our illustrious government irrevocably fixed. But if these things are permitted, if they who feel the impulse of duty to maintain the authority of government, are to be checked in their purpose by the false and infamous aspersion of servility, directed against them from rebels and conspirators; what becomes of conscious sincerity, of virtuous courage, of triumphant honour? Shall these be banished from the nation in accomodation of the scheme of treason? Shall the clamor of villany unnerve and paralyse the arm of integrity? Is not this the stale and hacknied artifice of crime wherever it appears? Has not the tyrant at all times challenged the assertor of liberty for a rebel; and has not the traitor at all times challenged the vindicator of government for a slave? And are these senseless words, uttered in rage and despair, to command the world and to break the spirit of freemen? It is our duty, a duty which honour no less than conscience peremptorily enjoins, to take our post between tyranny and treason; to resist with equal vigour and unrelaxing determination, the enemies of regulated liberty, from which ever side they advance; whether they insult under the style of Prince or of Citizen; whether they emblazon on their banners the Crown or the Cap; whether their pretext be, to reduce rebellion, or to extinguish tyranny: they are equally

and

and eternally the enemies of peace, of freedom, and of England.

At all times the defence of just government is the defence of right. The interest of the power of government, under the British constitution, is the personal interest of every free and upright Briton. It is the power that commands that state of outward circumstance, from whence results the enjoyment of every object of his right. At all times, therefore, interest and duty direct us, with the voice of authority, to maintain the constitution in all, and each, its parts.

But at this particular time, and in respect of those tragical events to which this address has reference, the duties of Englishmen, and of YOURSELVES most especially, are called forth in a peculiar manner towards that particular branch of the constitution, which has been more immediately endangered.

Those who are unable to discriminate between courage and ferocity, between religion and superstition, between the use and the abuse of things, we have no hopes of convincing that loyalty is not servility. But let such persons know, that the confusion of their own ideas will induce no confusion into the nature of things; and that none are so little likely to lapse into servility, as they who take pains to investigate the nature of loyalty, and to ascertain its extent.

"Allegiance," says the Law of England, "is
"usually, and therefore most easily, considered as
"the duty of the people; and protection, as the
"duty of the magistrate; and yet they are recipro-
"cally the rights as well as duties of each other.
"Allegiance is the right of the magistrate, and
"protection the right of the people.*"

"Allegiance is the tie, or *ligamen*, which binds
"the subject to the king, in return for that pro-
"tection which the king affords the subject.†"

"The law holds, that there is an implied, origi-
"nal, and virtual allegiance owing, from every sub-
"ject to his sovereign.—For as the king, by the
"very descent of the crown, is fully invested with
"all the *rights*, and bound to all the *duties*, of
"sovereignty, before his coronation; so the subject
"is bound to his prince by an intrinsic allegiance,
"before the induction of those outward bonds, of
"oaths, homages, fealty, which were only institut-

* Blackstone. B. I. c. 1.   † Ib. B. I. c. 10.

" ed to remind the subject of his previous duty,
" and for the better securing its performance.—
" Which occasions Sir Edward Coke very justly
" to observe, that all subjects are equally bound
" to their allegiance, as if they had taken the
" oath; because it is written by the finger of the
" law in their hearts, and the taking of the corporal
" oath is but an outward declaration of the same.*"

" It is due from all born within the king's
" dominions immediately upon their birth. For
" immediately on their birth they are under the
" king's protection; at a time too, when (during
" their infancy) they are incapable of protecting
" themselves. Natural allegiance is therefore a
" debt of gratitude, which cannot be forfeited,
" cancelled, or altered, by any change of time,
" place, or circumstance, nor by any thing but the
" united concurrence of the legislature.†"

" Allegiance is held to be applicable, not only
" to the political capacity of the king, or regal
" office, but to his natural person and blood royal.—
" And from hence arose that principle of *personal*
" *attachment*, and *affectionate loyalty*, which induced
" our forefathers (and, if occasion required, would
" doubtless induce their sons) to hazard all that was

* Ibid. † Ibid.

" dear

" dear to them, life, fortune, and family, in defence
" and support of their liege lord and sovereign."†

Thus speaks the free, but just and honourable, spirit of the constitution, by the pen of one of the ablest assertors of the rights and liberties of Englishmen. And the more we shall examine what it pronounces the more we shall discover, that every fair induction of reason, every genuine impulse of honour, will guide us to the same conclusion.

The protection to be thus afforded, to the subject, proceeds in a principal degree from the natural and mechanical exercise of the regal office; which is so contrived under that admirable form of government which we have in a general way considered; that the most common action of its own principles, if they receive no obstruction from him who is to exert it, furnishes a degree of protection to the subject, unknown in any other country. But if it happen that the individual exercising that office, at any given time, shall possess a mind harmonising with these principles, and shall add the impulse of his own inclination to the natural action of the springs, as opportunity shall offer; then the degree of protection is increased; and although the great majority of protection afforded, is to be

† Ibid.

attributed

attributed to the kingly office legally discharged, yet the access of protection is to be ascribed to the particular inclination of him who exercised it; and is, upon every principle of truth and ordinary justice, to be imputed to the individual himself.

What general protection has been uniformly extended to the nation, by the faithful discharge of the duties of the Crown; but in a more especial and striking manner, during the awful crisis of the present reign; during the paroxysm of seditious and fanatical fury in the year 1780; and again, during the last few years, in which the alarm that pervaded the nation has been gradually allayed by the wisdom and determination of parliament, and the daring enemies of the constitution coerced and reduced, by the firm and faithful exertion of the executive arm; is known and felt by all who are so happy as to possess their minds in freedom, unbiassed by the control of passion or of party. But to tell Englishmen that they enjoy the general protection issuing from the Crown through every subordinate function in the realm, would be an idle occupation of their time; it would be telling them of that which the experience of every parish in the kingdom, daily and hourly demonstrates. But to inquire whether we have received any particular
protection

protection from the opportunities afforded to the actual possessor of the Crown, and to be ascribed to himself, *personally*, on the principle above adduced, may not be so idle an occupation of their time; and it is one that honour and justice positively enjoin; because it is against him *individually* that passions the most infernal, acting by instruments the most formidable, have directed all their energy.

Personal liberty, is the great cry of Englishmen; it is the houshold god of every tenement in the realm; it is so deeply impressed upon our imaginations, that many while they actually possess it, run about in pursuit of it, with as much anxiety and as much jealousy, as if they had it not. It has been the policy of arbitrary sovereigns, in all times and countries, to preserve an influence over the courts of judicature, in order to ensure the execution of their will, and the coercion of those who might attempt to disturb its career. They did this, either by reserving to their own persons the power of determining causes, or by appointing to that office creatures of their own, instruments of their designs, and dependants on their pleasure. " In very early times, our kings (says Blackstone) " often heard and determined causes between
" party

"party and party." In the courfe of events, "they delegated their judicial power to the judges "of their feveral courts;" but ftill, as thefe held their fituations by the pleafure of the fovereign, and as the emoluments of thofe fituations depended on the fame pleafure, the door was open (as experience fhowed) to many and great abufes, and to various opportunities for fatisfying the appetite of the Crown, at the expenfe of the liberty of the fubject. To remedy this dreadful evil in fome degree, and to prevent the entrance of fo many abufes as that latitude admitted, a ftatute was enacted in the thirteenth year of WILLIAM III. by which the judges' commiffions were made out to continue during their good behaviour, their falaries were regulated, and other provifions were made, tending confiderably to reduce their dependance on the Crown. But though the door to abufe was thus nearly clofed, yet it was not entirely fhut; and while it remained in any degree open, abufes were ever liable to infinuate themfelves, and the perfect liberty of the fubject remained unfecured. Such was the cafe when his prefent Majefty afcended the throne of England; but———*fuch is the cafe no longer*. Hiftory will faithfully proclaim, and pofterity will gratefully commemorate, the illuftrious caufe of this laft act that remained, to clofe and rivet the perfect liberty of Englifhmen. It ftands stands thus recorded on a page, that will outlast every thing that is not immortal as the spirit of its author; that,

" BY THE DESIRE OF HIS PRESENT MA-
" JESTY, THE JUDGES HAVE BEEN MADE
" COMPLETELY INDEPENDENT OF THE KING,
" HIS MINISTERS, AND SUCCESSORS."*

" By the noble improvements of the law of
" 13. W. III. in the statute of 1. Geo. III. enact-
" ed at the earnest recommendation of the King
" himself from the throne, the judges are conti-
" nued in their office during their good behaviour,
" notwithstanding any demise of the Crown,
" (which was formerly held immediately to vacate
" their seats) and their full salaries are secured to
" them during the continuance of their com-
" missions; his Majesty having been pleased to
" declare, *That He looked upon the independence*
" *and uprightness of the judges, as essential to the*
" *impartial administration of justice; as one of the*
" *best securities of the rights and liberties of His*
" *subjects; and as most conducive to the honour of*
" *His crown.*†"

By thus obtaining the door to be finally closed against abuse, or undue influence, in the admi-

* Blackstone, b. iv. c. 33.   † Blackstone, b. i. c. 7.

niftration of juftice, to the prejudice of the liberties of the fubject, and by effectually removing the judges beyond the reach of royal or minifterial difpleafure, His Majefty has done that, which if told of fome hero of remote time, would have ftood foremoft in the catalogue of his deeds. Here then we believe, that juftice muft concede, that not only mechanical protection has been afforded by the Crown, but that this protection has been increafed by the caufe abovementioned; namely, the impulfe of inclination in a mind harmonizing with the principles of the conftitution, in the man actually adorned by the crown.

There is another kind of protection, not neceffarily flowing from the kingly office, however eminently becoming it, and that is, the protection, or general benefit and fecurity, refulting from the force of virtuous example. This, wherever it occurs, is perfonal and individual; it is the effect, not of human laws, not of artificial contrivance, but of an intrinfic regard to what is right, of an active principle, urging to the obfervance of that moral rule which the mind recognifes to be prefcribed by God. Whether or not fuch example is difplayed from the throne, let common fenfe, and common-place honefty pronounce. We fhall not make this appeal to cavillers and fcoffers thofe annoy-

annoyers of every thing grave and important, but to those who compose the great bulk of the nation; to all the different relations of husband and wife, of parent and child, of master and servant. Let every family be a tribunal to decide, whether domestic virtue is recommended from the throne, by the commanding power of example; whether the obscurest retreat affords an instance of nature's fairest ties more honoured or secured, than in the focus of artificial life, in the vortex of pleasure and extravagance? If the decision is affirmative, then let us look back to see, how often history teaches to expect the return of so great a blessing. What if the Court were a scene of profligacy and irreligion? What if we saw revived the dissolute times of Charles the Second? Should we not then, pursue in imagination, what we now in reality possess? Since, then, we have the protection of example held out from the eminence of sovereignty and with a lustre not often paralleled in the annals of our history, let us not be so despicably mean, as to withhold from it the honour due to it in every situation in life; nor so preposterously stupid, as to be unable to estimate its value in that particular elevation. Let us cherish the blessing we possess with all the anxiety that honour can inspire, and defend it with all the effect that wisdom can suggest; and when the course of nature shall occasion the niftration of juftice, to the prejudice of the liberties of the fubject, and by effectually removing the judges beyond the reach of royal or minifterial difpleafure, His Majefty has done that, which if told of fome hero of remote time, would have ftood foremoft in the catalogue of his deeds. Here then we believe, that juftice muft concede, that not only mechanical protection has been afforded by the Crown, but that this protection has been increafed by the caufe abovementioned; namely, the impulfe of inclination in a mind harmonizing with the principles of the conftitution, in the man actually adorned by the crown.

There is another kind of protection, not necefsarily flowing from the kingly office, however eminently becoming it, and that is, the protection, or general benefit and fecurity, refulting from the force of virtuous example. This, wherever it occurs, is perfonal and individual; it is the effect, not of human laws, not of artificial contrivance, but of an intrinfic regard to what is right, of an active principle, urging to the obfervance of that moral rule which the mind recognifes to be prefcribed by God. Whether or not fuch example is difplayed from the throne, let common fenfe, and common-place honefty pronounce. We fhall not make this appeal to cavillers and fcoffers thofe annoyers of every thing grave and important, but to those who compose the great bulk of the nation; to all the different relations of husband and wife, of parent and child, of master and servant. Let every family be a tribunal to decide, whether domestic virtue is recommended from the throne, by the commanding power of example; whether the obscurest retreat affords an instance of nature's fairest ties more honoured or secured, than in the focus of artificial life, in the vortex of pleasure and extravagance? If the decision is affirmative, then let us look back to see, how often history teaches to expect the return of so great a blessing. What if the Court were a scene of profligacy and irreligion? What if we saw revived the dissolute times of Charles the Second? Should we not then, pursue in imagination, what we now in reality possess? Since, then, we have the protection of example held out from the eminence of sovereignty and with a lustre not often paralleled in the annals of our history, let us not be so despicably mean, as to withhold from it the honour due to it in every situation in life; nor so preposterously stupid, as to be unable to estimate its value in that particular elevation. Let us cherish the blessing we possess with all the anxiety that honour can inspire, and defend it with all the effect that wisdom can suggest; and when the course of nature shall occasion the

the demise, may the impression of the example accompany the progress of the Crown, through every future descent!

"*The Rights of Man,*" with equal absurdity and insult, takes pains to signify to us that the king is a man; and to this sublime discovery, its disciples triumphantly subscribe. Miserable resource of impotence and spleen! The king is indeed a man like ourselves, placed in the most arduous and perplexing of situations. Are any so grossly dull as to think, that a king has more capacity for pleasure, less capacity for pain than another? that the proportions of happiness are bigger in him than in another? if any such should exist, the sordid scoffing of that libel will be converted into a salutary and useful instruction. The king is indeed a man, and it is from this common nature that result, the duties we owe to him, and that he owes to us. But while this herd assume great merit to themselves for thus reducing a king to the standard of a man, they perpetuate the distance they pretend to have effaced, by reducing themselves below the standard of men. For what can the mind conceive more absolutely below the character of men, than the mixture of ferocity and cowardice they at once display? what can be divised more dastardly, than to abuse the assured forebearance and temper of the executive arm, to the infernal purpose of destroying the life that might exert it; what more cowardly and ferocious at once, than with the genuine spirit of a Nero, to aim a death blow at the constitution in that part, where the political body becomes united under one head?

The king is indeed a man; one placed, for the public security and peace,* in that singular situation, a situation in which he can have no equal, consequently no friend, except it be upon the principle of loyalty. If loyalty be extinguished, let even the clumsiest feelings suggest what must be the situation of a king, of one especially whose powers of acting are limited and prescribed. The life of a king, of this country at least, does not consist of gold and purple, of pomp and enjoyment, of the chace or the theatre; envy or malignity must have corroded that man to the very core, whose mind can discern in the situation of a king, nothing but the outward accidents of splendor annexed to the office, (and therefore inseparable from the person), for the most reasonable of purposes; and whose imagination magnifies those satisfactions which the human nature requires according to its relative situations, into a state of perfect enjoyment, and emancipation from all concern. To be the perpetual butt and mark of ambition, disappointment, re-

* See this subject profoundly and honestly treated by the Republican De Lolme, b. ii. c. 2. & 10.

venge, obloquy, and scurrility; to live in the certainty of multiplying enemies in a compound ratio to any favour that the office must confer on some one; to pass an existence in the daily exercise of some part or other of the most weighty and embarrassing of functions; to feel in no single instance the perfect liberty of life, free from the necessities of ceremony or business; to be obliged to submit weekly to the afflicting duty of signing the doom of men; thus having scenes of crime, death, and distress, continually before the mind: these, and a thousand other considerations, evidently show, that the situation of a king, as it is in no degree an object for our envy, so neither is it a fit object for our hatred. The king, less than any other man, can make his personal interest the end of his acting. When therefore his person is endangered, he defends it as a public and not a private concern. But as public measures are not determined with the same rapidity with which private interests are pursued, but require deliberation and calculation of the bearings of different interests; he is often obliged to postpone the consideration of the kingly person that can die, to the dignity of the kingly office that cannot die. Here, then, is a favoury moment for the sanguinary appetite of treason. But how feels *loyalty?* or, in other words, how feel *justice* and *honour?* They impel to the succour of the prince; they sympathise with the feelings of the man;

they view him as brought into this diftinguifhed peril, from being foreman in their caufe; they refolve to fhare in that danger which the defence of their rights has occafioned; they anticipate the claim to allegiance, which the protection of thofe rights has eftablifhed; and they vie in each to form a phalanx round the man, in whofe perfon is fought, the diffolution of government, the enlargement of all crime, the plunder of all property, and the annihilation of the fyftem of our happinefs, raifed on the well-laid foundation, of the Englifh Conftitution.

Such ever was, fuch in a peculiar manner is at prefent, and fuch under parallel circumftances ever will be, the fuggeftions of native and unalloyed honour, even though it were never to be called by the name of loyalty.

Is it for Us deliberately to inquire, whether the fuccefs of the fcheme of regicide would in reality be attended by effects fo durable and extenfive? is it for Us to compute, whether, and how much, they have overrated its iffue; and to regulate Our correfponding fentiments by the cold rule of geometrical proportion? If it be fo, let *allegiance* be meted out by the ftricteft rule of *protection*; let it be iffued with the moft parfimonious attention to that

rule

rule, let mechanical protection receive only mechanical allegiance; let rational protection receive a rational allegiance; but let affectionate protection also receive from the breasts of Englishmen, that affectionate loyalty which none but freemen can bestow, and which our ancestors most liberally gave, when they grasped the sword in defence of their liberties.

Let this principle live, let the reason on which it lives be cultivated, and it cannot fail to prevent the return of those odious scenes which the present occasion retraces on our memory. If it should not enflame the hearts of those who at that time so deeply sold themselves to treason, it will at least inflame YOUR hearts, who occupy the capital, who constitute its strength and splendor, and who are equally interested in its honour as its safety. Let Englishmen feel their native value; let them feel, not only that the defence of the government is their duty, but that the protection of the constitution is their right; and if the protection of the whole be their right, so is that of those parts of which the whole consists. If the subject of the divan prostrates himself in the progress of his sultan, let him know that he bows before him whose property he is, who has power over his person and his life. But if the freeman of Britain shall escort the progress of the Crown, if he shall testify his loyalty by shouts and acclamations, let him know that he offers this tribute to one, who has no power whatever over his person or his life; but to him who is the ostensible head, and highest organ, of that constitution, from whence all his enjoyments and security proceeds; of that constitution, which is his native and unalienable birth-right, and in defending the distinct, constituent parts of which, he defends the sum and complement of all his happiness.

So truly is the government of England constituted in conformity with the laws of man's nature, that duty and right equally conspire in directing to its defence.

It appears, that a sense of the powerful union of these two principles, duty and right, urging to the defence of the constitution, has driven its enemies to employ all their abilities to separate the two, and having separated them, to endeavour to destroy, or prevent, the natural force of each. They fought to rob the constitution of the support it received, from the persuasion that it insures to every one the enjoyment of his natural right, by contending, that

the

the objects of that right, far from being comprehended by, are excluded from, the established system of English polity; so that the activity which a sense of right inspires, ought rather to be directed in subversion of such a system, than in its preservation. But, despairing of the success of so scandalous a falsehood, while the mind of man was undisturbed by passion, and capable of apprehending truth in its native form; they called forth a fresh exertion, and endeavoured to eradicate the motive of duty. They found, that the bonds of subordination could never be loosened, while the principle of duty continued to triumph over every other motive of action. They, therefore set themselves to enfeeble this principle; by persuading the interests and passions to believe, that it was a fiction of tyrannic birth, intrinsically hostile to the high and sublime notion of absolute right; which (they maintained) ought to be the first and governing motive in man. Thus sending God into the back ground, and rendering their actual gratification the leading consideration of their nature. This stratagem partially succeeded; still however the tree adhered to its native soil. They could not entirely eradicate it; for though they succeeded in bursting many of its roots, it still held firm by the strong tap-root of religion. As every principle of religion instigates to the discharge of duty, and therefore tends to confirm the fabric of civil government established, every such principle became adverse to their views in proportion to its vigour. But of all such principles of religion, the most completely and inexorably destructive of their endeavours was, the principle of christian religion; because it surpassed every other by the distinctness of its rule, the brilliancy of its evidence, and the power of the motive it affords. They observed, that those who really act in obedience to its impulse, act in the strictest parallel with the original direction of government, and act inflexibly: that they eminently consider *duty*, as the only rule for human acting: that they cannot be too minute in ascertaining that rule: that they deny the breach of any duty to be compatible with the establishment of any right: and that they estimate the affairs of earth as an object by no means fitting to terminate the speculations of the human nature. Here then was a force which, if government could attach it to itself, was superior to every power of resistance they could possibly oppose to it: it was a self-acting, a self-controlling principle, by which each would compel himself to do that, which government was contrived to compel every one to do. It is no wonder that they who laboured to defeat the end of civil government, and to emancipate the passions from moral control, should observe a principle of so fatal a tendency,

with

with extreme jealousy, aversion, and dismay: That they should fear beyond all things the inveteracy of such a principle; and should observe with alarm the vigour it might possess: that in proportion as it was strong and fixed, their enmity to it should increase: and that if they should any where discover it to be established on a basis that no human means could affect, that their rage and despair should be carried beyond all bounds. To this, then, as to the strong and towering fortress that defied all their attempts, and opposed the completion of their triumph, the great collected force of assailment was to be directed. Like those who exclaimed on seeing the last apparent obstacle of their desires; *come let us kill him and the inheritance shall be ours*; so argued these; *come, let us cut christian religion by the root, and the sublunary world is ours to rifle and despoil.*

Thus it was that,
―――" He, who envies now YOUR state,
" Who now is plotting how he may seduce
" YE also from obedience, that with him,
" Bereav'd of happiness, YE may partake
" His punishment."

He, who first endeavoured to rob us of all present enjoyment by his, " Rights of Man;" set himself with increased assiduity to subvert all our speculations gulations of a future happiness, by his, "Age of "Reason."

The adversaries of Christianity exhibit various degrees of acerbity and force, of bigotry and fraud. Experience, however, has happily shewn, that it is far from being as really dangerous to the interests of human society, as it is hideous to the mind, when the enemies of civil order and religion arrive at the last act of their desperation, and raise the arm against heaven. Though nature seems to blacken at the scene, the crisis is then past; man has done his worst. While the energies of man combat with their equals, the adversary may long preserve an appearance of equality, sometimes of superiority; but when at length he arrogantly presumes that he has exhausted the oppositions of earth, and throws out the gauntlet to heaven, there scarcely exists a mind so miserably depraved, as not to find the illusion instantly disappear. The true proportions of the quixote become instantly portrayed; and he who one while puzzled the imagination by the magnitude of his pretensions, now shrinks to the tininess of a mite, too small for any other affection, unless that of compassion, And though the heart may palpitate at the impiety of the assault, it yet

conceives

conceives no portion of alarm; on the contrary, the apprehensions that first possessed the fancy are now allayed, and the mind relapses into quiet by a consideration of the power provoked into the contest. We may venture to pronounce, that if the puny champion instead of coming singly, were followed by " the gates of hell," they would " prevail" nothing.

When the enemies of God and man have brought the battle to this issue, the warfare of man is closed. If man has faithfully defended that sphere that he was created to fulfil, God has undertaken the rest, and will confirm the interests of man. He has prepared an host invincible, ever ready and alert for such occasions; an host of evidence, brighter than the blaze of noon; and which are poured forth from the arsenals of truth, whenever the welfare of his servants demands it.*

It

---

* The arguments by which the truth of Christian Religion is upheld, have been invariably the same in every age, because in every age the same grounds of opposition have been urged against it. It stands therefore invincibly established, by the efforts of reason and learning, in each succeeding generation. The reader will find a most convenient summary of these in, Grotius, *On the Truth of Christian Religion.* Butler's *Analogy of Religion, natural and revealed, to the Constitution and Course of Nature.* Addison's *Evidences, &c.* Leslie's *Short and easy Method with the Deists.* Mr. Archdeacon Paley's *View of the Evidence of Christian*

It is impossible for the mind, on this occasion, not to recal that description which the poet so terribly paints, when the enemies of the eternal polity of heaven arrived at the period of their discomfiture, and,

" Stood reimbattel'd fierce, by force or fraud
" Weening to prosper, and at length prevail
" Against GOD and MESSIAH, or to fall
" In universal ruin last; and now
" To final battel drew, disdaining flight
" Or faint retreat, when the great Son of God
" To all his host on either hand thus spake.

" Stand still in bright array, ye Saints here stand
" Ye angels arm'd, this day from battle rest;
" Faithful hath been your warfare, and of God
" Accepted, fearless in his righteous cause;
" And as ye have received so have ye done
" Invincibly; but of this cursed crew
" The punishment to other hands belongs;
" Vengeance is his, or whom he sole appoints;
" Numbers to this day's work is not ordained
" Nor multitude; stand only and behold
" God's indignation on these godless poured
" By me; not you, but ME THEY HAVE DESPISED."

While the contest was of those matters which called for the vigorous exertion of the mind to

tianity: and in Bishop Watson's, *Apology for Christianity*, addressed to Mr. Gibbon; and his *Apology for the Bible*, addressed to Mr. Paine. To these, the reader may add, with satisfaction to himself, *The Jews' Letters to M. Voltaire*; and the celebrated M. Bonnet, of Geneva, on the Truth of Christianity: he will also find many of the arguments collected with the most pious and benevolent designs, in Sullivan's *View of Nature*, vols. v. vi.

vanquish

vanquish error, or establish truth, on points respecting man's nature, but which were involved in perplexity and obscurity, then was toil and fatigue, doubt and dismay. But, when the contest is turned to matters long since rescued from all perplexity or obscurity, and placed for ever in the full meridian of truth; when it is turned to heaven, and to the dispensations of heaven by which happiness both present and eternal has been dispensed to millions; then the labours of man cease; he is left free and unmolested; he needs only to direct his mental perception towards that blaze of evidence, which all those who are sincerely anxious to discern, have it always in their power to do.

Besides these, the more virulent and ferocious enemies of christian religion, there is another class, certain coxcombs of sophistry and sarcasm, on whom the courtesy of the world has lavished the title of philosophers; who triumph prodigiously, whenever they see their pigmy champions strutting in defiance of that colossal power, whom the wisest and best of men during eighteen centuries have worshipped, from the dawn of reason to the close of life, with unrepenting devotion, and with the most exuberant consolation. As a ferocious malignity seems to characterise the former, so a sneering malignity seems to characterise these. But they

they seem little aware of the nature of that ridicule to which they so familiarly recur. They appear not to have discovered in human nature, that the readiness with which laughter is excited by serious objects, is usually in inverse proportion with depth of penetration, extent of comprehension, or power of combination. Where a wise man discovers an object for serious contemplation, one of these can only glean a few scattered and unconnected matters, titillatory of laughter, and congenial with the weak flaccid texture of their minds. Let such philosophists know, that from the days of Sir Christopher Wrenn, myriads of little insects have passed their hours in detaching and removing particles of mortar, moss, perhaps of stone itself from the immense fabric of St. Paul's cathedral; yet have their little labours produced no sensible effect whatever on the solidity, magnitude, beauty, unity, or utility, of that most sumptuous structure. And just so the reptile instruments of sophistry and sarcasm, so busily employed against the far more stupendous fabric of christian religion, have worked for ages without producing any effect; unless indeed in the microscopic eyes of the insects themselves; the capacity of whose optics is not sufficient to embrace the entire form and proportions of that body, on which each one exercises his forceps or proboscis, in constant, but ineffectual, atrition. There have

have been those, who were able to notice in the convulsions of death, nothing but the **wry face**; there were also those, who while Socrates was imparting to the heathen world truths to them the most consolatory and sublime, could attend to nothing but his turned up nose. These were minute philosophers; men, gifted with the splendid faculty of abstracting the wry face and the turned up nose, from all the various confused objects presented to the heart and understanding. Of a similar complexion are they, whose mental powers are so constructed, as to be able only to discover in the cumbrous compound of scripture, those particular objects, which are best qualified to excite in them their venerable and characteristic affection of laughter.

It is a fact not very honourable to human nature, but standing on the faithful record of history, that in proportion as piety has increased in purity and energy by the promulgation of christianity, impiety has increased in malignity and intensity; and that in proportion as religion has, from the same cause, increased in weight and importance, irreligion has increased in levity and buffoonery.

" As the christian religion is adverse to the incli-
" nations and passions of the corrupted part of
" mankind

"mankind (says an admired writer) it has been
"its fate in every age, to encounter the opposition
"of various foes. Sometimes, it has undergone
"the storms of violence and persecution. Some-
"times, it has been attacked by the arms of false
"reasoning, and sophistry. When these have
"failed of success, it has at other times been
"exposed to the scoffs of the petulant. Men of
"light and frivolous minds, who had no compre-
"hension of thought for discerning what is great,
"and no solidity of judgment for deciding on
"what is true, have taken upon them to treat
"religion with contempt, as if it were of no con-
"sequence to the world. They have affected to
"represent the whole of that venerable fabric,
"which has so long commanded the respect of
"mankind; which, for ages, the learned have
"supported and the wife have admired; as having
"no better foundation than the gloomy imagi-
"nation of fanatics and visionaries."*

But if these are reflections qualified to give us pain, there is another which is qualified to give us the most substantial comfort; it is this, that the enemies of christian religion, of civil government, and of the English constitution, prove, in general,

* Blair. *On scoffing at Religion.* Vol. 3. Serm. 18.

to be one and the same. This is a reflection, that will remove any doubt we might have partially admitted; and it discovers to us, that if we will only be faithful, and not surrender up the interests of either of the three, each will confirm the other: Christian religion will impart unceasing energy to the true principles of civil government, and those principles will effectually sustain the fabric of the constitution. As civil government is a scheme to compel the discharge of *a part* of that obligation under which man is born, and as christian religion furnishes an impulse propelling and aiding each to discharge *the whole* of that obligation; it is evident, that the effect of christian religion, comprehends the effect of civil government, and anticipates its design; that it causes every man to govern himself more effectually than artificial government could do, and that it therefore, gives animation to all those principles on which civil government is established. And, again, as all sound principles of government; suppose the subjection of every constituent part of the state to the obligation of duty, and require therefore a reciprocal and equal action of the artificial force of government on all those parts, so as to be equal and complete in its effects on each; and as the constitution of England is the only government in point of practice, and the only system in point of theory, that can adduce a

satisfactory

satisfactory evidence of its ability to execute that great design with any degree of perfection, and to maintain that ability unalterably; it is manifest, that the genuine principles of government are reduced to their most fruitful experience, under the happy form of polity constituted in these kingdoms.

Others who despaired of altogether extinguishing christian religion, imagined the artifice of separating its present and future influence; and granted its excellency in respect of a future condition of the human nature, provided it might be conceded to them, that it was incompatible with the present unavoidable condition of human society; and they liberally allowed its spiritual pre-eminence, in order that they might obtain an acknowledgment of its temporal inferiority. This at least would reduce its consequence in respect of that compass of existence, which engaged all their concern. But here again they failed; for the duties of Christianity are duties in perfect unison with the original scheme of government; they are the complement of that uncertain rule, collected from the unaided light of reason, which constitutes what is called, the law of nature; and they so evidently proceed from the same common source, that if they were certainly fulfilled,

they

they would fupercede the neceffity of government; becaufe, as we obferved, each would then govern himfelf in a manner much more effectual, than any fcheme of human polity can poffibly govern any one. It was indeed incompatible with duplicity, with intrigue, ambition, violence, &c.; which belong, not to the ufe, but to the abufe of government. But it was not incompatible with the pure and genuine notion of government; fuch as every wife and good man underftands; and which demands an *equality of control* over the human fpecies, in order to provide for each an *equality of fecurity*. When this fallacious notion was promulged, and it was alleged, " that true Chriftians could " never conftitute a ftate capable of continuing:" the great Montefquieu replied, " And wherefore " not? They would be citizens inftructed, in an " eminent degree, in their duties, and moved by " an active zeal to difcharge them; they would " be able perfectly to comprehend the rights of " felf-defence; the more they felt themfelves " bound to their religion, the clofer they would " attach themfelves to their country. The prin-
" ciples of Chriftianity deeply engraven on their
" hearts, would be infinitely more efficient than
" the artificial honour of monarchies, the mere
" human virtue of republics, or the fervile fear of
" defpotic

" despotic governments*. Christian religion that
" commands all men to love each other, necessa-
" rily intends that every people shall possess the
" best political and civil laws attainable; because
" these, next to itself, constitute the greatest
" happiness that man can either receive or com-
" municate."† If peace, and the arts of social
life, can contribute to the continuance of a
state, such a state must continue; because it
be undisturbed by intestine commotion, and would,
as far, as it was possible, avoid all external hostilities.
" If Christian nations (says an ingenious writer)
" were nations of Christians, all war would be im-
" possible*." And what more would be required,
to bring back the human nature to the original
condition in which it proceeded from the hands of
its Creator, and to which the restorative dispensation of Christianity, is intended to reduce it
again?

Christianity reveals the whole scheme of man,
the origin of all his relations, and the end of all
his capacities. It expands the narrow sphere in
which philsophers had contemplated his nature,

§ *Esprit des Loix*, L. xxiv. c. 6.   † *Id.* Lxxiv. c. 1.
‡ Soame Jenyngs, *Int. Evid. of Chr.* p. 55

extending it on the one side to the eternal attributes of the Deity, and on the other to the eternity of duration. In this stupendous enlargement of the interest of man, the little sphere of duty that had employed the speculations of his reason, is lost and absorbed. The term of his present existence forms but a point of his total existence; the laws of his present nature, are but partial and transitory relations of his general nature; and the interests of this diminutive portion of his being, are in every respect subordinate to the interests of his perpetual duration. Under the Christian dispensation, man knows no governing or absolute rule, but the will of God; he knows no final object, but the eternity of his existence. As these are inseparable from the views of a Christian, they qualify the notions that a Christian forms of civil government. And they do this, not by introducing new principles subversive of those which are implanted in nature; but by extending those very principles to their full and perfect growth; thus fostering the weak and yielding plant, till it become a strong, towering, and umbrageous tree.

The absolute distinction between the law of nature and the law of revelation, exists only in the minds of those who make that distinction; and betokens, either inaccuracy of perception, that cannot ascertain the identity of an object; or narrowness of capacity, that cannot embrace its totality. Natural law, is the will of God, partially and confusedly collected, by the labours of the human reason; revealed law, is the same identical will, but perspicuously and distinctly exposed, by communication from God. They are one and the same object under different degrees of evidence; and in the degrees of that evidence, all their diversity consists. So that the moralist who should labour to determine the sum of man's obligation by the rule of natural law only, with the entire exclusion of the rule provided in the law revealed, would be like an astronomer, who should obstinately persist in determining the constellations or the planetary system, by the tube of Galileo, rather than by those of Huygens or of Herschel.

Those unbelievers in christianity, who disclaim all share in the characters above exhibited; and who, from living within the light of christian religion have been enabled to collect a system of religious ethics, agreeable to their reason, and to which a natural rectitude of heart inclines them; will do well, and consonantly with that rectitude, to ascertain exactly the source, from whence they have derived that exuberant store of truth, which disposes them very unjustly to infer, that christianity is superfluous, and therefore false. Jealous of reason, and not aware how anxiously christianity appeals to the bar of reason; hostile to superstition, and not aware how completely christianity dispels superstition; they have erroneously rejected in christianity, at once the vindicator of reason and the vanquisher of superstition. But let them be careful to certify to their minds, whether that beautiful system of morality which they admire, be not obtained through the aid of revelation;* whether that system be not comprehended in christianity, and whether it were known to mankind before its promulgation. And if, as is demonstrably true, the wisest philosophers were able to attain to it, till the diffusion of revealed truths enlarged the capacities of man, and defined his notions; then, let them be fair to acknowledge the magnitude of the debt in which they stand obliged to the luxuriance and munificence of christianity.

In proportion to the capacity and genius of writers on the subject of natural law, the boundaries of that science have been extended, and its identity with the law of revelation has been fully demonstrated.

* See, Ellis's, *Knowledge of Div. Things from Revelation, not from Nature or Reason.* 8vo.

" In universal society, under the presidency of God," (says a genius of the first order,) " every virtue is comprehended in the obligation to universal justice; and not only our external actions, but also our internal affections, are subject to that most distinct and certain rule; and he who reasons worthily of natural law, will take into his consideration, not only the establishment of peace with respect to man, but the acquirement of friendship on the part of God; the possession of which is an earnest of eternal felicity. We are not born for ourselves alone; but belong, in part, to our fellow-creatures, totally, to God*." Thus much for the rule of acting. " To overlook the circumstance of future life," (says the same writer) " which is inseparably connected with the divine Providence; and to remain contented with some inferior and subordinate degree of natural law, that can have effect even among Atheists, is to despoil that science of its most beautiful part; and to extinguish many duties relating even to this life†. To prefer a nominal immortality, or a posthumous fame, which are but sounds incapable of conveying any benefit to us, to a solid and substantial happiness; what is it but a splendid stupi-

---

* Leibnizii Op. Tom. IV. Part ii. page 281.   † Idem, p. 277.

" dity?

" dity ? The doctrine of natural law, as expounded
" by Christians, that is to say, by men truly phi-
" losophers, is far too sublime and capacious to
" measure every thing by the accommodations of
" this life*." So far for the end of our acting.
And the same great teacher thus ably and
wisely concludes his comment : " To sum up
" what has been said, we shall say in general, that
" the *end* of natural law is, the benefit of all who
" are subject to it; that its *object* is, whatever can
" affect the happiness of others, and is at the
" same time under our control; and finally, that
" its *efficient cause* within us is, the light of eternal
" reason, transmitted by the Deity into our minds.
" Which things from being so clear and simple
" I apprehend have appeared to some men as too
" obvious; and that they have therefore been in-
" duced to excogitate something more paradoxical,
" which might captivate by its appearance of
" novelty; not being sufficiently aware either, of
" the pregnancy of that which they rejected, or of
" the imperfection of that which they adopted.†"

Such is the extent to which the circumference of
natural law has been gradually enlarged, by the
light that Christian Religion has diffused. How

* Idem.   † Ibid, page 287.

equally and powerfully that light is diffused; how clearly it exhibits to all, the rule of acting by which men are bound to employ their faculties; how forcibly the end it proposes compels an observance of that rule; is best represented in the words of one of the brightest ornaments of our church and country. By means of that perspicuous apprehension of the great truths of religion, which the Christian faith imparts, " rustics and mechanics (says this affecting writer) do in true know-
" ledge surpass the most refined wits, and children
" prove wiser than old philosophers. A child can
" assure us of that, wherein a deep philosopher is
" not resolved; for ask a boor, ask a child educated
" in our religion, Who made him? he will
" tell you, God Almighty; which is more than
" Aristotle or Democritus could have told! De-
" mand of him, why he was made? He will tell
" you, to serve and glorify his Maker; and hardly
" could Pythagoras or Plato have replied so wisely;
" examine him concerning his soul, he will aver,
" that it is immortal, that it shall undergo a judg-
" ment after this life, that accordingly it shall
" abide in a state of bliss or misery everlasting;
" about which points neither Socrates nor Seneca
" could assure any thing. Inquire of him, how
" things are upheld, how governed and ordered?
" He presently will reply, by the powerful hand
" and

" and wife providence of God; whereas among
" philosophers, one would ascribe all events to
" the current of fate, another to the tide of for-
" tune; one to blind influences of stars, another
" to a confused jumble of atoms: pose him
" about the main points of morality and duty,
" and he will in a few words better inform you,
" than Cicero, or Epictetus, or Aristotle, or
" Plutarch, in their large tracts and voluminous
" discourses about matters of that nature. So real
" a property, it is of God's law, *to give subtilty*
" *to the simple, to the young man knowledge and dis-*
" *cretion.**"

Thus

---

* Barrow, *On the Virtue and Reasonableness of Faith*, Serm. II. In this wise, faithful, and persuasive writer, the reader (if he has not already the happiness of being familiar with him) will discover the *zenith* of that sphere, of which the author of the *Rights of Man* may justly be esteemed the *nadir*. From this great and good man, he will obtain a knowledge of the Deity capable of influencing to moral action; he wil discover the verity of Christian Religion, unconfounded with the adulterous growth of human artifice and superstition; he will discover, fairness and candor; sound and precise reasoning; profound knowledge of every subject he attempts to investigate, and faithful communication of all that knowledge; he will find, in short, all that is not to be found in the *Age of Reason*. Nor is this to be evaded by alleging the mutilated effigies of Religion, which that work exhibits in order to effectuate the seduction of weak and undiscriminating minds from belief in Christianity. That effigies, culled and purloined as it is from the works of Christian Philosophers, betrays the archetype from whence it was stolen; but how unlike its sublime original!

"—— As when the sun new risen
" Looks through the horizontal, misty air,
" Shorn of his beams; or from behind the Moon,
" In dim eclipse, disastrous twilight sheds!"

And

Thus is christian religion the exhaustless source of that principle of moral obedience copied after in civil government, and the want of which that scheme is intended to supply. It is the life that government, proceeding from principles implanted by God, aims to establish. For what does government intend, but the peace and welfare of mankind? And what does christian religion enjoin, but universal love to all mankind? And what is "*love*" but "*the fulfilling of the law?*" Christian religion is therefore the life which the human nature will live, when the necessities of human government shall cease, and man be ultimately and immediately subjected to the eternal monarchy of God. It is a

---

And yet this adventurous author thinks it prudent to affirm, that, "excepting the book of Job, and one Psalm, the Bible contains no instruction on the subject of the Creator." He indeed acknowledges, "*but I keep no Bible*; but even this can furnish no extenuation of that falsehood; because he has given us sufficient proof, that he once had borrowed one at least, in order to misrepresent its contents. It was (according to his own avowal) a casual circumstance only that induced him to give this credit to the Book of Job, and not its own internal evidence. He tells us, that he had entirely discarded that book among the rest, when he chanced to read in a Jewish writer that it did *not belong to the Bible*; and *then* he took it into favour. It will be no arduous task to show, from the points inadvertently conceded by "*The Age of Reason*," both the certainty of Christian truth, and the no less certain inconsequence and falshood of all which that rancorous libel comprehends. Nor will this latter receive the smallest support from the illiterate, coarse, and ignorant attempt at a defence, by by which "*a Deist*" has disgorged his crude, undigested malignity, on the truly Christian manual of that learned Prelate, who has compressed into a small compass a valuable store of antidote, to follow the poison so industriously diffused.

perfect

perfect life attempted to be lived among the imperfections of human society. It is the anticipation of that scheme of polity, of social intercourse, which will supplant the distractions of the present scene, and which the great apostle so sublimely intends when he says, *"Our form of social union exists in heaven."**

And shall we then relinquish such a religion to the defilement of its assailers? Shall we desert those principles of social intercourse producing government which were originally prepared by God, and which are therefore naturally invigorated by the genial influence of His own religion? And shall we abandon that splendid form of government, rising out of those principles, and nourished by the fostering care of wisdom, of virtue, and of freedom, during a growth of many centuries? We need not YOUR answer. YOUR determination is too distinctly foreseen. That form of government, is all YOU can in this life enjoy, towards obtaining those blessings, which the original law of nature, and the subsequent dispensation of christianity, design for the human species. But unless we manfully adhere to the post of duty; unless we display to the enemy a vigi-

---

* Ἡμων το πολιτευμα εν ϐρανοις υπαρχει PHILLIP. iii.20. The force of this passage is greatly enfeebled in our version, which renders it thus: "Our conversation is in heaven."

lance equal with his, and a courage and power superior to his; that blessing will be precarious and insecure. Of all mortal prognostics among states, none are so dreadfully certain, as imaginary security in the midst of danger. "*The kings of the earth, and all the inhabitants of the world, would not have believed that the adversary and the enemy should have entered into the gates of Jerusalem;*" And yet they did enter, and did "*not leave one stone upon another.*" To defend the constituted polity of England against its embittered and distracted foes, is at all times, therefore, the duty of Englishmen; to defend it at this particular time, or to stand prepared for its defence, is a duty in a peculiar and conspicuous manner imposed upon You; because Your Residence is the theatre that Treason has selected for her atrocities; and because the unquestionable light of experience discovers to us, which is The Occasion that she esteems most favourable to her views. What You are to do, how You are to conduct Yourselves, is not for us to presume to point out. The laws of your country impose a salutary constraint on the activity of individuals, and consign the power of all public acting exclusively to the organs of the state. But what those laws concede, that You may rightfully assume. And surely they concede to You various means for preventing the repetition of those scarcely paralleled enor-

enormities; which, at the time of the king's last progress to the Parliament, produced a transient comparison between the capital of England and the capital of France. You have wisdom, You have power, You have leisure to decide, how You may best oppose loyalty to treason, freedom to savageness, courage to ferocity, obedience to rebellion, order to disorder. All that we may venture to suggest is, in the words of the highest authority; *"Be vigilant.—Be strong and of good courage; dread not, nor be dismayed."*

Should treason, either in the head or herd, think this our effort worthy of aspersion; as an offering of superstition, a tribute of servility, a labour of venality, or a tool of tyranny; we shall give it no heed; but shall repose, with confidence and with security on the secret suffrage of the wise and the good.

THE END.

www.ingramcontent.com/pod-product-compliance
Lightning Source LLC
LaVergne TN
LVHW061214060426
835507LV00016B/1928

9 781535 814027